ROMAN BRITAIN

Gillian Hovell

This first edition published in Great Britain in 2012 by
Crimson Publishing
Westminster House
Kew Road
Richmond
Surrey
TW9 2ND

The right of Gillian Hovell to be identified as the author of this work has been asserted by her in accordance with the
Copyright, Designs and Patents Act, 1988.

ISBN 978 1 78059 077 6

Designed and typeset by Michael King

Printed and bound by Craft Print, Singapore

CONTENTS

INTRODUCTION

The Romans occupied Britain for 400 years and in that time transformed the country. Towns, forts, villas and roads appeared and daily life changed as new trade, social and political opportunities developed.

The ruins at Vindolanda

A ROMAN LANDSCAPE

Britain had been a rural world of timber-built houses and farms surrounded by a few hillforts, often echoing with the sound of tribal territorial battles (see p.12). The arrival of the Romans brought a revolutionary new way of life. The farming continued but now a new, foreign force was in power. The Romans built forts (see pp.52–61) from which they could expand their control and police their province. They also created new economic and social centres in the form of towns that housed several thousand people. The new towns were adorned with monumental public buildings (see pp.30–51) and, for the first time, Britain was criss-crossed by paved roads and the rich began to build grand stone houses on their farming estates (see pp.62–67).

 DID YOU KNOW?
The Emperor Augustus proudly proclaimed that he had 'found Rome a city of brick, but left it a city of marble'. The Romans did much the same for Britain but replaced timber with stone.

THE EXTENT OF ROMAN INFLUENCE

The changes introduced by the Romans occurred most readily in England, starting in the south where towns, and later villas, developed and grew. Wales and Cornwall, although conquered, remained on the fringes, adopting limited Roman styles and ways.

Northern England always retained the air of a military zone and its wealth depended on the army's spending power and the infrastructure and trading network it supplied.

WHO WAS IN CONTROL?

The rule of Rome, personified in the governor of Britain (see p.72), replaced the divided tribal lords (see p.13). Law and order was now enforced by the external might of the Roman army, stationed in forts throughout the land. If taxes and tribute were offered to Rome, all was peaceful but any resistance to Roman authority would be met by the point of the sword.

Julius Caesar first invaded Britain in 54BC

 DID YOU KNOW?
Emperor Augustus brought *Pax Romana* (Roman peace) to the known world but it was a double-edged sword: the Roman historian, Tacitus, invented a speech for the Caledonian tribal leader, Calgacus, at the battle of *Mons Graupius* (see p.23) in which he famously said the Romans 'create a desolation and call it a peace'.

 WEIRD AND WONDERFUL
Although we talk of 'Roman Britain', Scotland never truly adopted Rome's ways (Hadrian's Wall is a visible sign of the edge of the frontier) and Ireland was never conquered.

Statue of Emperor Constantine in York

A CHANGED BUT UNCHANGING WORLD

After the invasion in AD43, life in the new towns and villas very quickly became noticeably Romano-British: dress, home-life, education, politics, status and material possessions were all influenced by Roman culture (p.40). Once established though, relatively little changed, except that the frontiers in the west and (mostly) the north shifted and changed, and that the rush of stone building in towns became a way of boasting of wealth and status in the country villas.

IF YOU LIKED THIS...

There are many Roman sites to visit in Britain where we can explore Roman daily life. Exhibition centres at villas like Brading (see p.65) delve into home life, and museums on military sites like Arbeia (see p.59) show what life was like as a Roman soldier.

BUILDING ROMAN BRITAIN

Stone buildings were new to Britain but they spread within decades: forts with granaries and headquarters, and defensive walls, grand houses, temples, bath houses and the commercial and judicial centres of forum and basilica (see glossary) all appeared. The arenas of death – the amphitheatres – soon followed as places of social interaction and entertainment, and eventually the country villas became the most luxurious examples of Roman buildings in Britain.

WEIRD AND WONDERFUL

Romans had very different values to our modern way of thinking: amphitheatres were arenas for social interaction as well as violent entertainment.

GETTING ON IN LIFE

Daily life in pre-Roman Britain had been one of farming and fighting where warrior chiefs

The Emperor Hadrian

fought their way to the top. Rome was now in charge, but native Britons could improve their personal status through hard cash, earned by trade and skills, and the patronage (see glossary p.94) of a higher-ranking Roman.

The rewards of this social advancement included fine dining, new luxury material goods and elegant clothes, and perhaps a grand house with underfloor heating. All you had to do to succeed was to adopt Roman ways, pay your taxes and give tribute to the cult of the Emperor (see p.71). Even local beliefs and customs were respected by the Romans, although they were absorbed into a Roman form.

DID YOU KNOW?

The Romans introduced Britain to a society that was based on hard cash. It flowed from the coins that made up the soldiers' pay packets, and it spread into every corner of the province.

The benefits of the Roman Empire – trade, social status and freedom from inter-tribal wars – were open to all, as was education.

THE POWER OF EDUCATION

Pre-Roman Britain had been a completely illiterate society, but Rome was organised by a bureaucratic administration that was powered by written orders, decrees

The intricate mosaic at Fishbourne Palace

and correspondence. Everyone, from the native chiefs' sons who were taken to Rome to learn Rome's civilised arts and literature, to the lowest stall-holder who attached labels to the jars of goods he was selling, was expected to learn to read and write Latin. Legal issues, finance, military orders and everyday transactions promoted the social force that was the written word.

Roman Britain created a united province out of a land of feuding tribes. For 400 years, much of Britain was identifiably Romano-British. But what did that really involve, and how can we explore Roman Britain for ourselves?

The answers are in the sites that we can visit throughout Britain.

 IF YOU LIKED THIS...
You can see examples of Latin at most sites in Britain: inscriptions on military milestones and altars sit in museums beside potters' marks on Roman tableware. Personal letters at the fort of Vindolanda (see p.60) contrast with bronze tablets recording a soldier's retirement.

 DID YOU KNOW?
After the Roman invasion, Britons even took on Roman names. These were easier to use in the sounds and structures of the Latin language but also showed that the Britons had adopted Roman ways and considered themselves part of the Roman world.

ROMAN BRITAIN TOP 10

The Roman period is one of the richest sources of archaeological finds, sites and recorded historical events in Britain. They combine to give a wonderful glimpse of Roman life, its buildings, military might, personalities and treasure.

1 CLAUDIUS' INVASION OF BRITAIN, AD43

The real start of nearly 400 years of Roman rule in Britain. The invasion didn't just bring soldiers, it changed Britain into a land full of Roman goods, culture, town life, literacy and law and order. See p.16 for more.

3 BATH

Buried and preserved for centuries, this iconic site is awe inspiring, atmospheric and an essential place to visit. See p.38 for more.

5 BOUDICCA'S REVOLT OF THE ICENI, AD60/61

A bloody and violent rebellion against the conquerors. Fuelled by outrage, the destroyed cities and mass murder stretched the Roman army to the limit. Boudicca is the enduring image of resistance against Roman oppression. See p.20 for more.

2 GOVERNOR AGRICOLA

Immortalised by Roman historian Tacitus, Agricola was a governor of Britain who changed the shape of Roman Britain in just six years (AD77/8–AD83/4), pushing the frontiers further than ever before and encouraging building projects and the adoption of Latin. See p.75 for more.

4 THE BIRTHDAY INVITATION

A writing tablet discovered at Vindolanda contains a birthday invitation and is the earliest source of handwriting by a Roman woman anywhere in the Empire. See p.60 for more.

6 HADRIAN'S WALL

The Wall stretched from one side of the province of Britain to the other and it is still dotted with the solid remains of forts, milecastles and turrets. See pp.24 and 56 for more.

7 THE ROMANS REVOLUTIONISE LIFE IN BRITAIN

The Romans changed not just where people lived, but how they lived, where they worked, who they socialised with and how they impressed them, what they wore and what they ate, and how they spent their time. See pp.82–91.

8 ROMAN VILLAS

One of the most visible and exciting archaeological remains from the Roman period in Britain (see p.52). Bignor and others were home to Romano-British life at its most luxurious.

9 THE LEGACY OF THE ROMANS

Modern life owes much to the Romans. Our towns and architecture, our network of roads, our coins and our literature, even the words we use every day: if the Romans had never invaded we might have none of them. See p.90 for more.

10 MILDENHALL TREASURE

High quality silver treasure discovered in 1942 consisting of 34 items from the late Roman period. It includes the fantastically decorated Great Dish, covered with Bacchic figures and an elaborate central design. See p.89 for more.

TIMELINE

55BC
Caesar invades

AD43
Plautius

AD47
Chichester

AD50
Brading villa

AD60s
Bath

AD70s
York

AD77/78
Agricola

100BC	50BC	0	50AD	100AD	150AD

AD43
Claudius invades

AD47
Conquest of the South

AD60/61
Advance
into Wales

AD60/61
Boudicca's revolt

AD71
Conquest of
the North

AD77
Invasion of
Scotland

AD80
Wroxeter

AD85
Dover

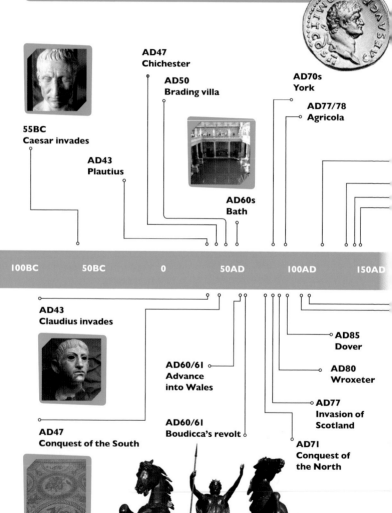

AD122
Hadrian's Wall

AD139
Antonine Wall

AD191/2
Albinus

AD410
Britain is released

AD117
Hadrian

AD140s
Bearsden Bath House

AD367
Barbarian attacks

150AD   200AD   250AD   300AD   350AD   400AD

AD306
Constantine

AD122
Nepos

AD205/7
Senecio

AD400
Romans begin to leave

AD100
Lullingstone villa

AD211
Britain is divided

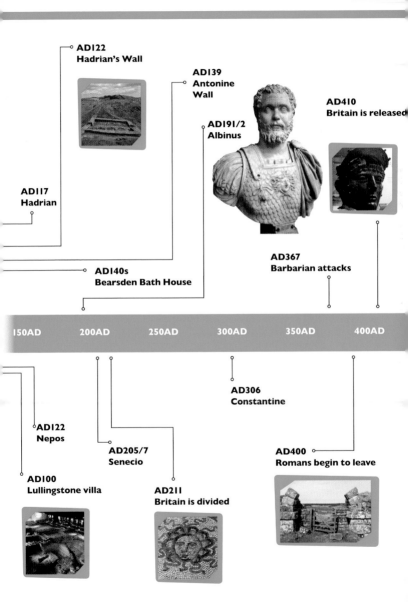

LIFE IN BRITAIN BEFORE THE ROMANS

Although Britain had links with the continent across the Channel, the Romans viewed it as another world, a dark land of barbarians and terrifying rituals. In reality, it was a divided and fierce tribal society.

Reconstruction of an Iron Age roundhouse at Butser Ancient Farm

A LAND OF RUMOUR

The Romans saw Britain as the northernmost part of the world, a land on the very edges of civilisation. The tales of barbaric rituals carried out in shady groves and of screaming, half-human savages petrified even the battle-hardened troops of Claudius in AD43. The Roman soldiers were paralysed with fear before they stormed the druids' powerbase on Anglesey in c.AD59.

THE REALITY

Of course, these rumours were only part of the story: the Roman accounts were good propaganda – the Britons needed taming, and the general who could do that must be a great man indeed.

Nonetheless, the archaeology shows that the Britons had their own culture. It was an illiterate one, and one largely controlled by the powerful druids (whose rituals included human sacrifice) but it included trade with Gaul and beyond by sea-faring boats. Despite the Roman ideas of barbarians there was a social structure that was sophisticated enough to plan and build major tribal defensive sites such as Maiden Castle in Dorset.

'Grain, cattle, gold, silver and iron... are exported from the island, as are hides and slaves and dogs that are naturally suited for hunting.'

Strabo, an ancient historian recorded exports from Britain in Geographica iv.2

A TRIBAL SOCIETY

Society was organised into tribes who each had their own ways: the Parisii are known for the archaeological remains of their 'chariot burials' in which the dead were buried with their chariots. The Iceni spread across Norfolk and into Suffolk and Cambridgeshire and, like the Ordovices and Silures who held much of Wales, fiercely resisted the Roman invasion (see p.19 and the story of Queen Boudicca).

The northern Brigantes (ruled by Queen Cartimandua but split by feuds) had a troubled relationship with Rome. However, the Catuvellauni (led by Cassivellaunus and later Tasciovanus and Cunobelinus) were extremely powerful north of the Thames and, with the Trinovantes, had links across the Channel, and were more inclined to adopt the benefits of Roman contact and conquest, as were the Atrebates in the south.

'The population is very large, their homesteads numerous in the land and the cattle plentiful.'
Julius Caesar in Gallic Wars v.12

POWER STRUGGLES

Despite the diverse tribal structure the Romans saw *Britannia* as a single unit, ripe for conquest. They called all the tribes in Scotland the *Caledonii*, but these 'red haired' and 'large limbed' (as described by Agricola and Tacitus) people included many other tribes. Likewise the Brigantes ('hill people', led by Queen Cartimandua) would come to mean all the tribes who stretched from the Irish Sea to the North Sea through Durham, Yorkshire, Cleveland and Lancashire.

DID YOU KNOW?

It has been estimated that over a million people lived in Britain when the Romans arrived.

STATUS SYMBOLS

The tribes controlled vast areas of land, and territorial disputes were a way of life in which warrior chiefs gained the highest status. These chiefs had the best of everything: while material goods for most were relatively limited, the chiefs' roundhouses might be filled with items fit for a king (or queen): wines brought from the continent and fine Roman plates were found even as far north as the Iron Age camp of Stanwick in Yorkshire.

IF YOU LIKED THIS...

Visit Butser Farm in Hampshire or Castell Henllys hill fort (used in the BBC's 1970s *Surviving the Iron Age* series) to see reconstructed Iron Age settlements and get a sense of what life might really have been like before the Romans.

THE ARRIVAL OF THE ROMANS

Trade had been flowing across the Channel for decades, but when Julius Caesar invaded Britain in 55BC and again in 54BC, he opened official contacts between the Britons and the Romans. By the time Claudius invaded in AD43, some tribes were already seeing that the Romans might have something to offer those who were willing to co-operate.

History

The history of Roman Britain spans 400 years from the conquest, through the expansion of the province and on into the later centuries of the Empire. Certain events mark key changes during this time.

THE CONQUEST

Julius Caesar's invasions in 55BC and 54BC (see p.15) paved the way for Claudius' real conquest in AD43 (see p.16). The decades that followed saw Roman soldiers march swiftly across England and construct a network of military strongholds. A series of campaigns took the Romans into Wales (see p.19), saw them deal with rebellions (see p.20), and move on up into Scotland (see p.23).

ALLIANCE AND ROMANISATION

Locals were eager to gain from trade with the soldiers who had wages to spend, and settlements grew up around the forts. As the legions moved on, some forts were demilitarised and soldiers retired in these newly founded towns.

In the north, the frontier advanced and retreated (see p.22) and Hadrian's Wall was built in AD122 (see p.24), closely followed by the Antonine Wall further north in AD142 (see p.25).

THE BEGINNING OF THE END

Command of the large number of Roman soliders in Britain tempted generals (who were high ranking politicians) to claim imperial power for themselves and so power in Britain was divided (see p.26), but various power struggles drew the army's attention away from Britain. Barbarians took advantage (see pp.25 and 27) and Rome eventually abandoned Britain to her own defences.

CAESAR'S INVASION

 DATE: 55BC–54BC | LOCATION: Deal, on the south coast of England
EMPEROR: Julius Caesar was joint ruler of the Empire with Pompey and Crassus

The first invasion of Britain was launched by Julius Caesar in 55BC, followed by a second in 54BC. First contact had been made.

AN INVITATION TO WAR

By 55BC, Britons were trading with Gaul (France) and were even supporting the tribes there in their war against Roman conquest. This was all the excuse Julius Caesar needed to start the first Roman invasion of Britain. Taking the 'barbarian' land of Britain would win Caesar political power in Rome.

THE ROMANS ARE COMING!

During the invasion two legions struggled to beach ships in the tidal waters and the Britons forced them to wade ashore, fully armoured, at Deal. Stalemate followed when a storm wrecked Caesar's fleet and the Britons refused to join a pitched battle (a battle at a chosen location). A defeated Caesar limped back to Gaul.

WEIRD AND WONDERFUL

The Britons wore nothing as they wielded swords, spears and shields against the armoured Romans. Instead they painted themselves blue with an extract of the woad plant to make themselves more frightening.

A SECOND INVASION

Caesar launched a face-saving invasion the following year and this time brought five legions and cavalry with him. At first the British tribes were shocked into co-operating under the leadership of Cassivellaunus, the powerful chief of the Catuvellauni tribe. However, pre-Roman Britain was seething with tribal disputes, and Cassivellaunus was soon betrayed and defeated. Caesar had won but he left to continue his campaign in Gaul and never came back.

'I see that there is nothing [in Britain] which we should either fear or which we should rejoice at.'

Cicero replying to his brother, Quintus' letters home from the invasion 54BC.

A bust of Julius Caesar

CLAUDIUS INVADES BRITAIN

DATE: AD43 | LOCATION: Southern England
EMPEROR: Claudius (AD 41–AD54)

Nearly 90 years after Caesar's invasion, a diplomatic incident gave the Emperor Claudius an excuse to send the general Aulus Plautius to invade Britain.

AN OPPORTUNITY

Although he was absolute Emperor, Claudius, like Julius Caesar before him, was looking for military success to improve his political position. Britain offered the opportunity for land, resources and the boost to Roman morale that expanding the Empire brought. In addition, his predecessor, Caligula, had raised two legions for an invasion of Britain that never took place – the soldiers needed to be kept busy.

The opportunity came when Verica, heir to the Atrebates' tribal throne, asked for Claudius' help after he had been forced out by Caratacus, chief of the Catuvellauni tribe in 40AD (see p.13 for more on the tribes).

WEIRD AND WONDERFUL

The Roman troops were fearful of crossing to the barbaric lands of Britain. Claudius had to send his freedman (a freed slave), Narcissus, to persuade them to set sail. The humiliation of having an ex-slave tell them what to do shamed the soldiers into obeying their general's orders.

THE INVASION FORCE ADVANCES

Claudius ordered Aulus Plautius to invade (under the pretence of helping the Atrebates tribe) and he landed 40,000 soldiers at Richborough, Chichester and one other unknown site in AD43. They pushed on and crossed the River Medway with the help of 'Celtic' auxiliaries (ancient historian, Dio, doesn't say who they were). The commander Vespasian marched west too – when the Iron Age Maiden Castle (Dorset) was excavated it was found to

Claudius exploited Britain for political gain

The Roman army had to be persuaded to enter Britain

be smothered with Roman catapult bolts from this invasion.

THE TRIBES TUMBLE

By AD40 the powerful Catuvellauni tribe had gained control of vast areas north of the Thames and the leaders Caratacus and Togodumnus, led the tribe against Rome. Togodumnus was killed but Caratacus fled west to Wales to lead the Silures and Ordovices tribes (a future thorn in Rome's side, see p.19). After such great leaders had been defeated, other tribes began to surrender. The Roman army quickly and violently conquered southern Britain.

DID YOU KNOW?

Within a few years of the invasion, Cunobelinus, King of the Catuvellauni tribe, issued coins in which he sported a Roman style helmet – Roman influence was already showing.

THE EMPEROR'S TRIUMPHAL ENTRY

After defeating the local tribes, Aulus Plautius waited with his troops in the marshy territories outside the Catuvellauni capital, Colchester (*Camulodunum*) for Emperor Claudius himself to arrive to lead the army to victory.

WEIRD AND WONDERFUL

Claudius brought war elephants with him to attack Colchester. Romans knew that the smell of them terrified enemy horses.

A huge classical temple was erected, containing a life-sized bronze statue of Claudius – worship of the Imperial Cult (see p.71) was required by all: refusal indicated a rejection of Rome itself. Rome had taken control of Britain.

DID YOU KNOW?

Claudius spent only 16 days in Britain before returning for his Triumphal Entry into Rome but he did name his son Britannicus in celebration of his success.

CONQUEST OF THE SOUTH

 DATE: from AD47 | **LOCATION:** Southern England and London
EMPEROR: Claudius (AD41–AD54)

Following Claudius' invasion, the south of England adopted Roman ways and towns developed. However, as Roman expansion continued, the armies were kept occupied in the west and the north with tribal uprisings.

SPREADING THE EMPIRE

The governor of Britain, Publius Ostorius Scapula (AD47–AD52), was based in Colchester with the *XX* Legion and he led them north and west to the unsettled frontiers. Meanwhile Vespasian (the future Emperor) took the *II Augusta* Legion to the south west, while the *IX Hispana* Legion headed north and the *XIV Gemina* Legion marched into the Midlands.

By AD47, the Romans controlled England from the River Humber to the estuary of the River Severn.

THE DEVELOPMENT OF TOWNS

As the troops headed north out of Colchester, retired veteran soldiers remained and settled down with their families in the old fort and became farmers. This Latin-speaking, thoroughly Romanised community was granted the status of *colonia* (colony of veterans). Traders and those seeking new lives or personal advancement joined them and more houses and public buildings quickly sprang up.

By the AD50s Roman towns such as *Londinium* (London, see p.37) had grown up around centres of far-reaching trade, and towns such as *Verulamium* (St Albans) and *Calleva Atrebatum* (Silchester, see p.33) had developed out of existing local settlements. Rome was here to stay.

Hod Hill houses an Iron Age hill fort

 IF YOU LIKED THIS...
Visit Hod Hill in Dorset and see the ramparts for the Roman fort built into the north west corner. Managed by the National Trust the site is open to the general public at all times.

ADVANCE INTO WALES

 DATE: AD51 | LOCATION: Wales and the druids' base on Anglesey
EMPEROR: Claudius (AD41–AD54)

While the south of England was adopting Roman ways, the north of England and the Welsh borders were fighting back. Years of campaigning occupied the armies.

THE ADVANCE CONTINUES

Publius Ostorius Scapula began his governorship of Britain (AD47–AD52) by suppressing a revolt of the Iceni in East Anglia before heading north and west.

Caratacus (the Catuvellaunian leader whom Plautius had defeated in AD43) had escaped west and now led the Welsh Silures and Ordovices tribes against Rome. Defeated again, Caratacus now fled to Cartimandua, queen of the northern Brigantes tribe. However, in AD51 she handed him over to Rome. Nonetheless, the Welsh resistance continued with relentless guerrilla warfare, and when Scapula died in AD52 it was said that he died of exhaustion.

The defensive walls of Caer y Twr Hillfort

WEIRD AND WONDERFUL

According to Tacitus the Roman soldiers were terrified when faced with 'black-clothed women with dishevelled hair like Furies, waving torches' and druids 'screaming awful curses'.

GOVERNORS GALORE

After Scapula's death Aulus Didius Gallus, an experienced general, was rushed in as governor and his presence swiftly ended the Silures' rebellion in Wales. However, Cartimandua, queen of the Brigantes, was feuding with her husband, Venutius and this power struggle occupied Gallus and his troops until he left the governorship in AD57.

PAULLINUS

Gaius Suetonius Paullinus arrived in AD58 and this most notorious governor of Britain began by storming Wales and destroying the power of the druids (who held control over judicial and religious aspects throughout the land) by wiping out their stronghold on Anglesey.

BOUDICCA'S REVOLT

 DATE: AD60/61 | LOCATION: Colchester, St Albans and London
EMPEROR: Nero (AD54–AD68)

Despite the conquest of Wales there were still uprisings and in AD60, Queen Boudicca led the Iceni tribe in revolt. Rome's command and her towns had to be rebuilt while a fresh power struggle grew in the north.

OUTRAGE

When Prasutagus, King of the Iceni, died in c.AD59, he left half his kingdom to the Emperor Nero in a bid to enable his queen, Boudicca, to keep the rest. However, the Imperial

A burnt pot found in Colchester

Procurator (head of finances in the province) Catus tried to win favour with Nero by forcefully taking everything. He then made things worse by demanding loans back and allowing the army to seize provisions. Boudicca resisted, for which she was flogged (whipped) and her daughters raped. The Iceni and Trinovantes tribes rose up in outrage.

DEATHS BY FIRE AND SWORD

By the time governor Paullinus returned from wiping out the druids in Anglesey (see p.19), Boudicca's rebellion had driven out the IX Legion, burnt Colchester, London and St Albans to the ground and massacred the populations. Tacitus, the Roman historian, wrote that 'there was no form of savage cruelty that the angry mob refrained from' and it is thought that as many as 70,000 people died in the revolt.

WEIRD AND WONDERFUL

The destruction led by Boudicca was so extensive that archaeologists can trace the revolt by the burned 'black earth' layer in the ground, and smashed tombstones in Colchester.

REGAINING CONTROL

Outnumbered, Paullinus and his advance guard could only retreat and watch the devastation from camp. The rebels, weighed down by stolen goods, were finally defeated when the Roman infantry caught up.

Boudicca herself escaped but died almost immediately afterwards. It is thought Boudicca poisoned herself but she may have been murdered.

Paullinus kept the soldiers mobile, policed East Anglia heavily, and quickly rebuilt the towns.

DID YOU KNOW?

Roman historians, Dio and Tacitus, writing after Nero's reign, both record Boudicca's revolt in reluctant terms of admiration: she represented the qualities of courage and loyalty that the current Emperor, the insane Nero, had lacked.

TROUBLE AT THE TOP

The incompetent Catus was replaced by Classicianus, who quickly established his grand palace in London, and criticised governor Paullinus, who was recalled from Britain in AD61.

DID YOU KNOW?

Classicianus' gravestone was found reused in fourth century fortifications in Trinity Square in London in two fragments (found separately in 1852 and 1935).

PERSONAL ANIMOSITIES

The new governor, Turpilianus, worked closely with Classicianius to rebuild south east Britain and its relations with Rome.

In c.AD63 Maximus succeeded Turpilianus as governor but Maximus feuded with Roscius Coelius, the Legate (commander, see glossary) of the *XX* Legion. When civil war broke out after Emperor Nero's death in AD68, the Roman army mutinied and, in AD69, Maximus fled Britain.

LOVE AND WAR

Vitellius, one of the four short-lived emperors of AD69, appointed Bolanus as governor of Britain and he continued a policy of appeasing the tribes. When Cartminandua, Queen of the Brigantes, took her husband Venutius's aide, Vellocatus, as her lover, the tribe rose up against her but the Romans helped her to escape, leading to anti-Roman feeling in the north.

A statue of Boudicca poised for battle

CONQUEST OF THE NORTH

**DATE: AD71 | LOCATION: Northern England
EMPEROR: Vespasian (AD69–AD79)**

Following Rome's assistance of Cartimandua, the aggrieved King Venutius led the Brigantes in a rebellion. Meanwhile the Roman army headed north and west to Wales.

THE BRIGANTES SUBDUED

After the Romans helped Cartimandua escape from the Brigantian power struggle in c.AD68/9, Cerealis spent his governorship years of AD71 to AD74 ending the Brigantes' resistance to Rome. His experience as Legate of *IX Hispana* Legion during Boudicca's revolt (see p.20) 10 years earlier was perfect training for this hard-fought campaign.

DID YOU KNOW?

King Venutius may or may not have faced the Romans for the last time at the hillfort of Stanwick: the theory is based on a few archaeological finds (such as fine pottery and amphorae of wine) fit for a king and the vast size of the Iron Age fort.

HEADING NORTH

While Romano-British life was thriving in the south, Cerialis was occupying much of northern England to prevent further unrest. Wherever the army went, so did the Roman network of defences and communications – forts (like Castleford, Yorkshire) were built in the north, leading to a spread of Roman control.

Remains of the Roman amphitheatre at Caerleon, Wales

Cerialis may have brought the *II Adiutrix Pia Fidelis* Legion with him to replace the recalled *XIV* Legion (now called *Martia Victrix* 'Warlike and Victorious' for putting down Boudicca's rebellion). He stationed them in Lincoln, thus releasing the *IX* Legion who pushed on towards York where they founded the first timber fortress there.

WALES CONQUERED

Frontinus replaced Cerialis as governor in AD73/4 and he campaigned against the troublesome Silures tribe in Wales. The fortresses at Chester and Caerleon were founded and Frontinus' solid campaign was completed by Agricola who succeeded him as governor in AD77/8. All resistance in Wales now ended and Rome's attention could again turn to the north.

THE INVASION OF SCOTLAND

DATE: AD77 | LOCATION: Northern England and Scotland
EMPERORS: Vespasian (AD69–AD79); Titus (AD79–AD81); Domitian (AD81–AD96); Nerva (AD96–AD98); Trajan (AD98–AD117)

Governor Agricola took the Roman army further north than they had ever been – and ever would reach again – all the way to the north east tip of Scotland. Unfortunately the success was only temporary.

ROMANS DEFEATED IN SCOTLAND

By AD81, the Romans had reached the River Clyde and the River Forth but, as the marching camps advanced up the east coast of Scotland, the uncontrollable Caledonian tribes joined forces and in AD82 the IX Legion was almost destroyed by a surprise attack.

MONS GRAUPIUS

The Romans won a decisive battle at the unknown site of *Mons Graupius* (AD83), but Emperor Domitian recalled Agricola, meaning the half-finished fort at Inchtuthill (Perthshire) and forts such as Strageath and Fendoch were dismantled. Rome abandoned northern Scotland.

This ceremonial helmet is on display in the National Museum of Scotland

Meanwhile in southern Scotland, forts such as Newstead were enlarged and new ones such as Glenlochar were built in a road-linked military network.

THE EMPIRE RETREATS

The Caledonian tribes, divided and uninterested in Roman values, were uncontrollable: in c.AD100, forts in southern Scotland were abandoned and Rome's frontier was pulled back to the Stanegate road and forts on the Tyne-Solway line.

WEIRD AND WONDERFUL

The Roman army often destroyed their forts and surplus supplies when they retreated. 160kg (353lb) of unused iron nails were found deliberately buried at Elginhaugh (Lothian).

BUILDING HADRIAN'S WALL

 DATE: AD122 | LOCATION: Northern England, Solway to the Tyne
EMPEROR: Hadrian (AD117–AD138)

Following Rome's retreat from Scotland in AD122 work began on Hadrian's Wall on the orders of Emperor Hadrian. It stretched 73 miles from the Tyne in the east to the Solway in the west.

WHY WAS THE WALL BUILT?

Emperor Hadrian visited Britain in AD119 as part of his grand tour of the Empire. The Wall established the northern frontier of the Empire in Britain but Hadrian had just been in Germany, where he had been shocked by the sloppiness of the troops and this may have inspired him to order the Wall to be built, as a way of returning some discipline to the army.

The Wall was not a simple barrier: forts, milecastles and turrets, regularly spaced along its route, controlled movement both into and out of the Empire.

Nepos, as governor of Britain (c.AD122–AD124) and a personal friend of the Emperor, was given the job of commanding the building of the Wall.

THE LANDSCAPE OF HADRIAN'S ROMAN BRITAIN

While the north and west frontiers remained a military zone where Caerleon, Chester and York housed three legions, southern Roman Britain had now developed into a land of flourishing towns

A substantial section of Hadrian's Wall still exists

and farmsteads, with roads and industries making luxury goods easily available. Tribal warfare had been replaced by status, comfort and even security.

 IF YOU LIKED THIS...
Check out how the Wall was built on p.56 and explore the sites along this amazing monument, such as Housesteads Fort (p.58).

ANTONINE WALL AND BARBARIAN ATTACKS

 DATE: AD139 | LOCATION: Northern England and southern Scotland
EMPERORS: Antonine (AD138–AD161); Marcus Aurelius (AD161–AD180);
Commodus (AD180–AD192)

Hadrian's Wall was the northern frontier for 20 years until the Antonine Wall was built further north in c.AD139–AD143. When barbarians poured over it in the AD160s, Rome retreated.

A NEW WALL

In AD139, Emperor Antoninus Pius (Antonine), seeking personal and political glory, ordered Urbicus, governor of Britain (c.AD138–AD142) to build a 63km (39 mile) wall of turf (a common Roman military defence fortification) with supporting forts further north than Hadrian's Wall, to stretch between the Firth of Forth and the Firth of Clyde.

 DID YOU KNOW?
In AD143 Antonine celebrated his conquest of southern Scotland with a series of coins depicting victory over Britannia, who is represented as a woman sitting by a shield. This design still appears on some coins today.

ATTACKS ON THE WALLS

In AD163, barbarians forced Rome to retreat to Hadrian's Wall. A few outpost forts directly north of Hadrian's Wall, such as High Rochester and Risingham, remained, but any forts further north were dismantled or (as at Drumlanring and Strageath) completely destroyed to

Part of the Antonine Wall

prevent the enemy using them.

In AD184, in the reign of the increasingly insane Emperor Commodus, barbarian tribes crossed Hadrian's Wall causing a huge amount of damage.

ROMAN CIVIL WAR

The unsettled Roman army mutinied and even tried to make their Legate, Priscus, Emperor (he declined). In AD192 when news of Commodus' murder reached them, governor Albinus (see p.77) weakened Britain's defences by taking most of Britain's garrison to Gaul in his fight against Septimius Severus to become Emperor. The British troops were a daunting imperial political weapon and, after Albinus was defeated in AD197, steps were taken to weaken control over it.

BRITAIN IS DIVIDED

 DATE: Early third century (AD211/2) to fourth century (AD307)
LOCATION: England | **EMPERORS:** Septimius Severus (AD193–AD211);
Caracalla (AD211–AD217); Postumus (AD260–AD269); Diocletian (AD284–
AD305); Carausius (AD286–AD293); Constantine I (AD307–AD337)

During a century and a half of leadership clashes in Rome, Britain was divided into two provinces, led by rebel Emperors, and later split into four provinces.

SEVERUS VISITS

From AD205 a vast rebuilding programme transformed the north of England as the Emperor Septimius Severus was coming to Britain with his sons, Caracalla and Geta, to reconquer Scotland. Severus died in York in AD211 during the campaign and Caracalla promptly killed his brother and left Britain to wage war in the East and in Germany.

DIVIDE AND RULE

To avoid leaving the British troops under one man's control, Britain was divided into two provinces: *Britannia Superior*, ruled by one governor in London, and *Britannia Inferior* ruled from York.

Rebel Emperors (men who just declared themselves Emperor) like Postumus and Carausius led to the division of Britain into four provinces c.AD312, to discourage future would-be Emperors.

 DID YOU KNOW?
In AD260, the British, Gaulish and Spanish armies supported Germany's governor, Postumus, when he proclaimed himself Emperor. Britain became part of his new Gallic Empire until his murder in AD269.

While Diocletian was Emperor, Carausius (the commander of the British fleet) declared himself Emperor of Britain and Northern Gaul in AD286. He ruled from Britain and restored Roman culture but was murdered in AD293.

PEACE AT LAST

In AD305, Diocletian (who was ill) and Maximian abdicated. Galerius and Constantius I became *augusti* but Constantius died in York in AD306 and, although Galerius had appointed two *Caesars*, the army in York declared Constantine to be *Caesar* and, in AD308, *augustus*. Constantine won sole command of the entire Empire in AD324.

Constantine brought stability to Britain

BARBARIAN ATTACKS

 DATE: AD367 | LOCATION: Northern England
EMPERORS: Valentinian I (AD364–AD375); Valens (AD364–AD378)

The next century was a constant struggle both against barbarians from the north and from raiders across the Channel.

BARBARIAN CONSPIRACY OVERRUNS NORTHERN BRITAIN

During Constantine's time in power, Britain enjoyed a period of peace and the rich continued to invest in luxuries for their villas. However, after he died in AD337 Britain's troops were often taken abroad for the almost constant imperial power struggles and, in AD360, barbarians took advantage of the shortage of manpower and charged over Hadrian's Wall. They raided northern England, seizing goods and prisoners. Military commanders Fullofaudes and Nectaridus were captured and Nectaridus was even killed.

RESTORING ORDER

In AD367, joint emperors Valentinian I and Gratian sent Count Flavius Theodosius to restore order in Britain. He arrived in Richborough and marched to London, catching barbarians loaded down with loot, returning it to its rightful owners, and releasing their prisoners.

Magnus Maximus was a well-respected leader

Army deserters were pardoned, and towns and forts were restored.

BRITAIN'S PLACE IN THE EMPIRE

Despite Theodosius' efforts though, Britain's defences against the barbarians were once again weakened: Magnus Maximus, a Spanish commander in the British garrison, proclaimed himself Emperor in AD383 and took troops from Britain to the continent to confirm his claim. Britain was being abandoned.

DID YOU KNOW?

Despite draining Britain of resources and troops, Magnus Maximus seems to have been a popular hero and Welsh Dark Age royalty claimed their family lines went back to a mythical Welsh King called Macsen Wledig, who may be identified with Maximus.

THE ROMANS BEGIN TO LEAVE

> DATE: AD400 | LOCATION: Throughout Britain.
> EMPERORS: Honorius (AD395–AD423); Constantine III (AD407–AD411)

A vastly reduced British army was fighting against the raiding barbarians but Britain's defences were thinned still further when a general, Stilichio, took control and removed still more soldiers.

A VANDAL TAKES CHARGE

In AD395, Honorius, a 12-year-old boy, inherited the Western Empire including Britain. Stilichio, a general who was born in Germany, acted as regent for the young Honorius. As 'Master of the Soldiers' it was Stilichio's job to protect Britain from the barbarian attacks. He began well enough but he soon withdrew more troops from Britain to fight the Visigoths on the frontiers in Germany.

DID YOU KNOW?

Because the *civitates* (citizens) of Britain were Roman citizens, they had the right to expect military support against attackers.

A SYMBOL OF HOPE

In AD406 Constantine III was proclaimed Emperor in Britain, just like Constantine I had been declared Emperor there in AD306. However, like many before him, he took the Roman army and its commander away from Britain to Gaul to fight to establish a new Gallic Empire of Britain.

Without legions in Britain, coins no longer arrived to pay them. Astonishingly, although this lack of coinage ruined Britons' spending power, Roman life struggled on in the villas and, in a reduced condition, in the towns.

BRITAIN ABANDONED

By AD409, Honorius gave in to Constantine III's military tactics and made him joint consul of Rome. Even when Constantine had achieved this legitimate control in the West, and although Britain was officially in his care now and he was duty bound to protect her, he still failed to return troops to Britain to defend her against a major Saxon invasion.

Above: Burgh Castle, a Roman fort built to defend Britain against Saxon raids

BRITAIN RELEASED FROM ALLEGIANCE TO ROME

 DATE: AD410 | LOCATION: Throughout Britain
EMPERORS: Honorius (AD395–AD423); Constantine III (AD407–AD411)

In AD410, officials in Britain asked the Emperor Honorius for help against barbarian invaders. He wrote back that he had no troops to spare. Britain was on her own and Roman rule of Britain was ending.

BRITAIN IS RELEASED

Constantine III had failed to be the hero Britain hoped for and his command was collapsing. Britons abandoned Roman authority and threw out imperial officials, breaking the formal links with Rome. If Rome could not help, then they would rule themselves.

Honorius had no manpower to defend Roman Britain: his troops were occupied with Goths and Vandals who were overrunning the continental frontiers – the Goths even took Rome in AD410. When Britain wrote, asking him for help against the Saxon invaders, Honorius wrote back telling them to 'look to their own defences'.

BRITAIN'S LAST HOPES

In AD449 the British leader Vortigern resorted, in the absence of help from Rome, to inviting two barbarian brothers, Hengest and Horsa, to bring a force of Angles and Saxons to deal with the barbarian invaders. They succeeded but then turned on the Britons and yet more Angles and Saxons invaded. Roman rule had been pushed out and a new Anglo-Saxon era was beginning.

Dorchester villa fell into ruin

Ambrosius Aurelianus, probably a descendant of the Roman aristocracy in Britain, brought peace for a while when he defeated the Saxons at Mount Badon in c.AD493 but the Saxons soon overpowered him.

 WEIRD AND WONDERFUL

The stories of King Arthur originate from the days of Aurelianus – as one of the last of the Roman aristocracy, could he be the model for the King and his knights?

THE END

In AD577, the Saxons won a battle at Dyrham, near Bath, and then seized Gloucester, Cirencester and Bath. The towns first established by Rome were now Saxon.

Roman Britain had ended.

Towns

The Romans introduced Britain to the concept of towns. Rome had a specific understanding of what a town should contain and how it should be organised. A town's status often depended on its origin.

DEVELOPMENT OF TOWNS

Towns were unknown for the Britons before the Roman invasion. Previously, sprawling concentrations of fortified settlements called *oppida* (the nearest Latin word Julius Caesar could describe them with) had lacked the organisation of a true town.

An *oppidum* might become a Roman town and remain a *civitas* (regional centre) of a tribal area. This was reflected in its Latin name, like Aldborough's name *Isurium Brigantium* which meant 'of the Brigantes'.

Many Roman towns grew out of a *vicus* (civilian settlement) around a Roman fort, while other towns, such as Colchester, Gloucester, York and Lincoln, started as actual Roman forts: when the legion moved on, some veteran soldiers would retire and settle down with their families.

WHAT A ROMAN TOWN WAS EXPECTED TO CONTAIN

Every Roman town modelled itself on Rome. Public buildings were essential but only some towns could hope to have public baths, an amphitheatre, a theatre, and a selection of shrines and larger temples, including one to the imperial cult (see p.71).

Laid out in an organised grid-pattern, towns were planned to have an obvious forum (open space for market and business) with a basilica (administrative and legal centre) at one end.

They were bustling, cosmopolitan trading centres, with shops and industrial quarters and good communications through channelled gates along paved roads and on to other towns.

LOCATIONS

1. Chichester
Noviomagus Reginorum

2. Silchester
Calleva Atrebatum

3. Colchester
Camulodunum

4. Canterbury
Durovernum Cantiacorum

5. London
Londinium

6. Bath
Aquae Sulis

7. Caerwent
Venta Silurum

8. Carlisle
Luguvalium

9. York
Eboracum

10. Cirencester
Corinium Dobunnorum

11. Wroxeter
Virconium Cornoviorum

12. Leicester
Ratae Corieltauvorum

13. Lincoln
Lindum

14. Dover
Dubris

15. Gloucester
Glevum

The town was usually serviced by running water from aqueducts and drains and, in time, city walls became a regular feature.

HOW THE TOWNS WERE ADMINISTERED

Every town was subject to the governor and ultimately the Emperor but otherwise it was self-administrating. A council of pro-Roman locals had control but each was expected to produce money for the town's benefit.

A *colonia* was a settlement of veterans/ Roman citizens in a demilitarised fort, and a *civitas* had higher status than a *municipium* (such as St Albans) whose residents were granted reduced Latin citizenship. However, when Caracalla (AD211–AD217) granted Roman citizenship to all in AD212, such distinctions became a mere technicality.

Towns promoted a Roman identity, and provided security and a vibrant social and economic environment.

31

CHICHESTER

LATIN NAME: *Noviomagus*
DATE FOUNDED: *c.*AD47
OTHER LOCAL ROMAN SITES: Fishbourne Palace; Silchester town
CURRENT STATUS: Continuous settlement since the Romans

Chichester existed as a Celtic settlement before the Roman conquest of AD43. Some of the earliest signs of Romano-British life have been found here.

EARLY ROMAN INFLUENCE

Chichester's Latin name, *Noviomagus* (New Market) echoes the name of the original Celtic settlement. There may even have been a very early (even pre-invasion) Roman fort at Gosbecks – could Roman troops have been sent to help a local chief? Roman influence is seen in a gold ring inscribed 'Tiberius Claudius Catuarus' – the Celtic name with two Roman forenames attached indicated this man had accepted Roman citizenship.

A ROYAL TOWN

The nearby richly-decorated Fishbourne villa was probably the palace of Cogidubnus (Togidubnus), the pro-Roman local King. The army moved out of the fort and it was turned into a grid-patterned timber-built town (still remembered in Chichester's North, South, East and West Streets).

TRADE AND INDUSTRY

The town council made a dedication to Nero in AD59 and trade flourished in this harbour town which was linked by a Roman road to the iron mines on the South Downs. In *c.*AD80 the town acquired an amphitheatre for animal

The intricate mosaic floor at Fishbourne Villa

baiting and gladiator fights and, later, rich stone-built houses with mosaics, glass windows and heated floors were built.

 DID YOU KNOW?
Chichester's walls were rebuilt and added to; in the late second century earthen ramparts with stone gateways enclosed the town but in the early third century, the ramparts were replaced with local flint. In the fourth century bastions were added and can be visited today.

SILCHESTER

LATIN NAME: *Calleva Atrebatum*
DATE FOUNDED: *c.*AD49
OTHER LOCAL ROMAN SITES: London; Bath
CURRENT STATUS: Completely abandoned but the city walls remain

Silchester had been an *oppidum* (Celtic proto-town) as far back as 20BC but it developed into a fully-fledged Roman town before being abandoned when the Romans left Britain in the early fifth century.

THE TOWN DEVELOPS

From AD49, the Romans developed the town first in timber, then in stone. By the end of the first century there was a large *mansion* (an inn for official visitors) and public baths. An amphitheatre – one of the earliest in Britain – was built in the north east of the town and could seat 7,000 people. In the second century, the town had an average-sized forum (1,720 sq.m. or 18,514 sq. ft.) and a grand basilica.

However, relatively few houses were built in stone. Timber structures remained popular, despite a terrible fire which meant the city had to be rebuilt in the late third century. Many industries flourished and it seems that the forum was used by metalworkers by the mid-third century. By then, stone walls over 6.3m (20 ft) high enclosed the town which covered an area of 43 hectares (106 acres).

THE END OF SILCHESTER

The Romans filled in the wells and abandoned Silchester in the early fifth century and only the impressive walls (and the restored amphitheatre) remain visible. Extensive excavations were made in 1864–78 and 1890–1909 but modern

digs continue to give us more information about life in this Roman town.

 DID YOU KNOW?
Silchester's Latin name, *Calleva Atrebatum*, meant 'Wooded Town' 'of the Atrebates tribe'. The use of the tribe's name shows that this remained an administrative centre for the region in Roman times.

The striking walls at Silchester

COLCHESTER

LATIN NAME: *Camulodunum*
DATE FOUNDED: Became Roman *colonia* by AD49
OTHER LOCAL ROMAN SITES: Multiple sites in London
CURRENT STATUS: Continuous settlement since the Romans

Colchester in Essex is situated north of the Thames and was the site of Emperor Claudius' Triumphal conquest. The fort built here was the first to be turned into a veterans' *colonia*.

THE BEGINNINGS

The Roman name, *Camulodunum* (the fort, *dunum*, of the Celtic god, *Camulos*) reflected a pre-Roman stronghold of the Trinovantes tribe, later occupied by the Catuvellauni.

THE EMPIRE STRIKES

The King of the Catuvellauni, Caratacus (son of Cunobelinus), drove out Verica, the King of the Atrebates in AD40. Verica appealed to the Romans for help and thus gave the Emperor Claudius the excuse he needed to invade (see p.16).

DID YOU KNOW?
Cunobelinus, King of the Catuvellauni, was Shakespeare's *Cymbeline* in his tragedy of the same name.

Emperor Claudius himself, complete with elephants, led the victorious invasion of *Camulodunum* in AD43. The Romans immediately built a fortress for the *XX* Legion on nearby high ground. The legion soon moved on to further the conquest of Britain but retired veterans stayed on with their families in adapted barrack buildings. The settlement that grew in the grid-patterned fort was granted the status of *colonia* by AD49 and honoured with a monumental arch at the west gate and the name *colonia victricensis* (city of victory).

'To Tiberius Claudius Caesar Augustus. . . the senate and people of Rome grant this [arch/inscription] because he received the surrender of 11 kings of the Britons, conquered without loss, and he first brought the barbarian peoples across the Ocean under the authority of the Roman people.'

Reconstructed inscription on Colchester's triumphal arch

CLAUDIUS THE GOD

The Roman Emperor expected to be worshipped as a god during his lifetime and for temples and statues dedicated to him to be built throughout the Empire. At Colchester, the impressive podium (still standing 3.5m/11 ft 6 inches high) on which the temple stood was later used as the foundation for Colchester's medieval castle.

One of the striking mosaics at Bignor Villa

TERROR

The Romans confidently flattened the old fort's walls but when Boudicca attacked during her revolt in AD60/61, the town was burnt to the ground.

 ### WEIRD AND WONDERFUL

A haunting life-size bronze head of Claudius, broken from a statue in the revolt, was found by a young boy in the River Alde in 1907. It can be seen in the British Museum in London.

LIFE IN ROMAN COLCHESTER

Before being burned down in AD60, Colchester boasted a senate house and theatre. By AD65 a city wall had been built and the town was being resurrected.

Trade flourished and in c.AD160 a fine pottery industry began and lasted 100 years. Even Chinese silk reached Roman Colchester.

By AD200, wealthy residents owned large townhouses and luxury country villas

were scattered outside the town.

Anglo-Saxons rapidly took over the crumbling town in the fifth century and Roman stones would be used in building in later years.

 ### IF YOU LIKED THIS...

Visit nearby Bignor Villa: its museum contains glimpses of life in Colchester, including a child's set of toy figures of a Roman dining party.

ARCHAEOLOGICAL CHALLENGE

Because Colchester is a modern town, excavation beneath it is difficult and limited. The 250m (820 ft) long chariot-racing stadium – the only one of its kind known of in Britain – was only discovered in 2004/5.

 ### IF YOU LIKED THIS...

Although the remains are hidden, you can still see the lines of the Roman walls and the grid pattern of Colchester's streets.

CANTERBURY

LATIN NAME: *Durovernum Cantiacorum*
DATE FOUNDED: c.AD40s
OTHER LOCAL ROMAN SITES: Richborough fort; Dover lighthouse
CURRENT STATUS: Modern town with a few Roman ruins

The Romans took over the existing Celtic settlement here in the AD40s and turned it into a major Roman centre that flourished for 400 years.

A BLEND OF CULTURES

The Latin name of this Roman *civitas* capital, *Durovernum Cantiacorum*, reflected the local name of 'alder swamp' 'fort' 'of the Cantiaci tribe'. This mix of cultures continued after the Romans took over in the AD40s, with classical Roman architecture sitting next to Romano-Celtic temples.

THE CITY CENTRE

Fragments of a theatre (dating from c.AD80–AD90 but enlarged and grandly redeveloped by the beginning of the third century) show that it was a sophisticated 70m-wide, four-storey building with circular vaults that created a raised auditorium. The town must have had a forum and basilica but they remain undiscovered, probably buried beneath the modern high street. Excavations are limited due to the modern town but they hint at a fine town centre that sported fluted columns with carved Corinthian capitals (decorative stonework at the top of the column), and Italian marble veneers.

A LASTING LEGACY

Although the Roman town declined in the fourth century and was largely abandoned when the Romans left Britain in the early fifth century, Canterbury became a Christian centre after the Romans left.

 IF YOU LIKED THIS...
You can track down the remains of Roman Canterbury in the fragments in Quenin Gate. Pieces of the once grand theatre lurk in the cellar of the Slatters Hotel, while the bath's hypocaust can be found in the basement of Waterstone's bookshop in St Margaret's Street. The rippling mosaics of a villa also sit beneath the Roman Museum.

A reconstruction of Roman Canterbury

LONDON

LATIN NAME: *Londinium*
DATE FOUNDED: c.AD49
OTHER LOCAL ROMAN SITES: St Albans; Colchester
CURRENT STATUS: Continuous settlement since the Romans

London was founded by the Romans and has been a centre of trade and business for 2,000 years.

BUILDINGS FIT FOR A CAPITAL

Founded in approximately AD49, by AD50 a Roman bridge had been built across the Thames (close to the modern London Bridge). Boudicca's revolt destroyed *Londinium* in AD60, but governor Classicianus based himself in the town by AD62 and the town was quickly rebuilt and improved. An amphitheatre seating 8,000 people was built by AD70, public baths by AD85, and a vast palace (at Cannon Street) by the end of the century.

A modest forum and basilica (AD75–AD85) were replaced by an imposing Great Basilica (probably the largest building in Roman Britain) during Hadrian's reign (AD117–AD138).

DID YOU KNOW?

According to Tacitus by AD60 London 'was not distinguished by the title of colony but was famous for its copious traders and commercial traffic'.

LONDON'S BURNING

Tightly packed wooden buildings lined streets in the first and second centuries but a fire in c.AD125–AD130 meant the city burned to the ground and had to be rebuilt.

The old Roman city wall still stands in London

MIXED FORTUNES

Carausius (AD286–AD293) made London the capital of his rebel Empire and struck his coins here, creating London's first mint. A massive third century fortified wall enclosed 138 hectares (341 acres), making *Londinium* home to something like 30,000 people, the largest city in Britain. Huge bastions were added to the walls in the mid-fourth century but London was in decline: the Great Basilica had been demolished by c.AD300 and houses were thin on the ground. Nonetheless, London survived to the end of the Roman period and beyond and was never abandoned.

IF YOU LIKED THIS...

Visit the Museum of London which gives the whole history of London from Roman times.

BATH

LATIN NAME: *Aquae Sulis* | **DATE FOUNDED:** By AD60s
OTHER LOCAL ROMAN SITES: The line of the Fosse Way
Roman road heads northward; Cirencester; Gloucester
CURRENT STATUS: Continuous settlement since the Romans

The Roman town of *Aquae Sulis* never had any formal status but was home to one of the most multicultural populations in Roman Britain. It contains the only Romano-British classical temple known in any detail.

THE GREAT BATHS

The hot springs in Bath were sacred to the local goddess, Sulis, and the Romans were quick to relate her healing properties to those of their own goddess, Minerva. Roman soldiers stationed at a (lost) fort on the nearby Roman road (the Fosse Way) were probably responsible for building a pool at the spring in the first decade after Claudius' invasion in AD43.

By c.AD60s or AD70s a new temple dedicated to Sulis-Minerva and the enormous baths complex were built. This massive complex of temples and baths

The goddess Minerva

became not just the centre of the town which grew up around it, but one of the most imposing of Roman ruins in Britain.

COSMOPOLITAN COMPLEX

While much of the great temple remains buried beneath modern Bath, the carved pediment (a low-pitched triangular stone gable on columns at the front of temples) that stretched across the front columns is a fine example of merged styles and cultures and of the absorption of local beliefs into Roman religion: although carved decades after Rome's invasion, the fiery, wild-haired gorgon on the pediment is distinctly Celtic.

 DID YOU KNOW?
The Latin name for the town, *Aquae Sulis*, means 'the waters of Sulis'.

AN ENGINEERING CHALLENGE

By the late second century, the heat and damp rising from the hot spring had caused the roof supports of the first baths to rot and they were reinforced and replaced by a vaulted roof – the massive piers can still be seen.

WEIRD AND WONDERFUL

A centurion of the region, Gaius Severius Emeritus, put up an inscription when he rededicated a 'sacred spot' in the temple precinct after it had been 'wrecked by insolent hands'. Vandalism, it seems, is nothing new.

MORE THAN JUST BATHS

The Roman walls enclose a mere 12 hectares (29.7 acres) but a much larger settlement grew up around it. The temple complex itself was a site for both leisure and for healing (an attribute of both the springs and the goddess Minerva). A temple of Mars (the god of war) stood nearby and a theatre would have been the centre of religious processions and performances. Standard public baths were part of the great temple-baths complex.

DID YOU KNOW?

The main spring (now called The King's Bath spring) bubbles up out of the ground at a staggering rate of a quarter of a million gallons a day and the water is a constant 46.5 degrees centigrade.

ROMAN RELIGION

The artefacts found here provide a valuable window into Roman religion: offerings of plaques, worn coins and prayers have all been found. Curses written on lead record the day-to-day concerns of Roman people between the second and fourth centuries – theft of clothes left while bathing was a daily concern and a frequent occurrence.

The Roman baths are an extremely popular tourist destination today

WEIRD AND WONDERFUL

Curses were simply prayers to the gods and in Roman times were as normal as prayers for a good outcome. Horrible illnesses, lack of sleep or even death were wished on the guilty thief until such time as they returned the stolen goods.

HOW DID THE BATHS SURVIVE?

The sheer scale of the buildings in Bath helped to preserve them – later Saxons admired them as the work of 'giants'. However, when the springs were no longer managed, the ruins became buried in protective silt and mud. Much of the Roman site remains inaccessible, buried beneath modern Bath – the full site must have been even more imposing in Roman times.

WHAT LIFE WAS LIKE UNDER THE ROMANS

The arrival of the Romans changed life for many people in Britain. Now there were new things to own, new homes to live in and new expectations in life. Both home and work were transformed.

FOLLOWERS OF FASHION

To be anyone of note in Roman Britain you had to show you were Roman: speaking Latin and having social airs and graces financed by hard cash improved your status.

Roman fashion demanded a long tunic for the women and a short tunic with a toga over it for the men. Quality jewellery, and oils and skin creams stored in delicate ornate glass bottles were all used to create the right image.

HOME SWEET HOME

Within decades of the arrival of the Romans rectangular Roman houses replaced most of the native roundhouses.

Hypocausts were used as underfloor heating systems

Home interiors were a matter of social pride: the latest mosaic designs and wall paintings were displayed with pride at dinner parties along with the best tableware you could afford.

IF YOU LIKED THIS...

Visit Fishbourne Palace and look out for the black and white geometric designs that peek out from the mosaics with pictures and colours. These colourful mosaics were laid over the black and white designs to keep up with the latest fashion.

TOWN LIFE

Many people were drawn by commerce and social opportunities into a new 'civil' life in the Roman towns. Although status was once acquired through tribal power, in the new Roman towns it could now be gained through wealth, patronage (the support of a higher-ranking Roman) and political office. Daily visits to the public baths (in town or outside the forts) provided opportunities for business contacts as well as relaxation, exercise and gossip.

Everyday Roman life was imbued with religion (see p.70 for more) and temples were a focus for local events.

An amphitheatre event was the ultimate Roman experience, including fashionable crowds, souvenirs and refreshments, cruel spectacles involving animals, criminals or gladiator slaves, as well as vast displays of wealth by the organisers.

WEIRD AND WONDERFUL
Hair styles (some highly time-consuming) changed as fashions came and went. Roman women even curled their hair using tongs heated in the ashes of a fire.

A TASTE OF ROME
Being part of the Roman Empire gave access to a whole new way of eating: high-ranking Romans brought expectations of a wide range of vegetables, meats and fruits.

DID YOU KNOW?
The Romans introduced Britain to many vegetables: celery, peas, turnips, radishes, asparagus, garlic, onions and cabbages now improved the British diet. New herbs such as rosemary, thyme, bay, mint and basil also began to be used to flavour meals.

COUNTRY LIFE
Very few towns had populations of more than 10,000 people and most Britons still lived in the country and worked on the land, but the Romans brought innovation here too. More productive grains and new varieties of cultivated fruits and breeds of livestock were introduced.

Industries such as metalworking and potteries grew up everywhere and tapped into new skills as well as the vastly

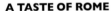
Public baths were used in daily life as a place to relax and socialise

increased market — everyone could now travel and trade via the new Roman roads that had been built.

LORDS AND MASTERS
The Britons now had to answer to the Roman officials who ran the province and who were supported by the Roman army. Although slavery was nothing new — prisoners from pre-Roman tribal wars became the victors' slaves — Roman slaves, were unique in the ancient world because they could earn their freedom or be freed in a master's will.

If you paid your taxes and tribute to Rome, life was stable, and farmers, tradesmen, merchants and even slaves could hope to make something of their lives. Education was encouraged from the beginning (especially by Agricola, see p.75) and literacy in Latin was a necessity for any political advancement.

However, no British-born official ever extended his influence beyond the British shores, indicating that Britain lacked the niceties of other Roman provinces.

Towns

CAERWENT

LATIN NAME: *Venta Silurum*
DATE FOUNDED: c.AD75
OTHER LOCAL ROMAN SITES: Caerleon fort and amphitheatre
CURRENT STATUS: Continuous settlement since the Romans

A small roadside town, Caerwent was created to house the defeated Silures tribesfolk. It never became a significant town but it did benefit from being granted the status of a *civitas*.

A TOWN FOR THE LOCALS

Governor Frontinus subdued the Silures tribe in the AD70s and, as Caerwent's Latin name, *Venta Silurum*, indicates, the Roman town was set up as the *civitas* of their region. It was surrounded by a massive earthen rampart and ditch and, unusually, the military Roman road that ran from the Roman *colonia* (town) at Gloucester to the fortress at Caerleon divided the town – a way to parade the glories of Rome before the locals. Few residents ever aspired to Roman finery though – mosaics and hypocausts are rare and outlying rich villas non-existent.

ROMAN ASPIRATIONS

The town, however, did have public baths, and a basilica that was decorated with carved Corinthian capitals and statues. The town can now boast the best preserved basilica and forum in Roman Britain, however, the open piazza of the forum was one of the smallest in Roman Britain, at only 1,023 sq.m. (11,011sq. ft.)

Impressive city walls were built in the late second/early third century – parts of them still rise to 5m in height today – and substantial bastions were added in the mid-fourth century.

 DID YOU KNOW?
The Roman baths were not just for getting clean, they were a social habit, a daily meeting place for friends and business acquaintances, as well as a space for leisure and exercise in the open *palaestra* (exercise yard). Caerwent's *palaestra* is unusual as it had a roof: a necessity perhaps in the British weather.

The remains of the once imposing Caerwent Wall

CARLISLE

LATIN NAME: *Luguvalium*
DATE FOUNDED: AD70s
OTHER LOCAL ROMAN SITES: Hadrian's Wall; Stanwix
CURRENT STATUS: Continuous settlement since the Romans

Carlisle fort was built in AD72 as the Romans advanced north. A *vicus* developed alongside the fort and thrived on the soldiers' spending power.

EARLY EVIDENCE

Carlisle's fort guarded a strategic river crossing where the main north to south road met the Stanegate road (a fortified route that ran from Carlisle to Corbridge in the east). Excavated alder tree timbers date the fort to the winter of AD72/73. However, by the time the fort was refurbished in AD83, the Romans had control of the north and brought in heavy oak beams.

AN UNSTABLE FRONTIER

By AD87 the Romans had retreated from Scotland and the Stanegate road became the northern frontier (see p.23). The fort was dismantled and then completely rebuilt in AD105 when the frontier proved too insecure.

A new timber fort, *Uxelodunum* (Stanwix), was built as part of nearby Hadrian's Wall in the AD120s. It was rebuilt in stone in the AD160s, as was the original Carlisle fort in the early third century.

DID YOU KNOW?
A milestone was found in Carlisle bearing an inscription, calling Carausius (the commander of the British fleet who set himself up as a rebel emperor of the north from AD286–AD293) *Emperor Carausius Pius Felix Invictus Augustus* (Holy, Blessed, Unconquered Augustus/Caesar).

CIVILIAN COMFORTS

Seventy acres of civilian settlement straddled the River Eden and was granted *civitas* status in c.AD209. Inscriptions in Greek as well as Latin show that this was a sophisticated diverse settlement, and that a *collegia* (guild) of stone masons operated here – the only British one known so far. Carlisle survived well (coins were found in ongoing repair sites from the AD380s) long after other Roman sites were becoming derelict – and St Cuthbert visited in AD685 and was proudly showed the working Roman aqueduct.

YORK

LATIN NAME: *Eboracum*
DATE FOUNDED: AD70s
OTHER LOCAL ROMAN SITES: Aldborough
CURRENT STATUS: Continuous settlement since the Romans

York's fortress was founded in AD71 and a busy civilian settlement grew up on the opposite bank of the River Ouse. The Roman fort was often upgraded as a base worthy of imperial visits.

THE BEGINNING

Governor Cerealis founded the fortress at York in AD71 for the *IX* Legion as a secure base for his campaign against the unruly Brigantes tribe. By AD107, the army was building stone gates in the fortress walls and setting up stone inscriptions. York was one of three legionary fortresses (with Carlisle and Lincoln) in the north and west military zone when Hadrian visited in AD119.

DID YOU KNOW?

Stonegate and Petergate streets run along the lines of the main streets of the fort.

The 10-sided multangular tower

SEVERUS IN YORK

York's defences were upgraded about the time of Emperor Severus' visit to Britain from AD208 to AD211. Some timber houses were replaced by stone houses which may have been built for the imperial family. At the same time, the Legate of *VI* Legion, Claudius Hieronymianus, set up an inscription for a temple to the Egyptian god Serapis in c.AD190–AD210. This coincided with the imperial visit by Severus who is known to have been fond of the cult.

WEIRD AND WONDERFUL

Gold trinkets have been found in a massive stone sewer that ran under York and survives under Church Street. They seem to have been dropped by ladies in the bath house.

YORK PROMOTED

Severus died in York on 2 February AD211. He had split Britain into two provinces (see p.26) and York became the capital of *Britannia Inferior* (northern Britain). The city was later granted *colonia* status.

'He died at Eboracum in Britain, having subdued the tribes which seemed hostile, in the 18th year of his reign, struck down by a very grave illness, being now an old man.'

The Augustan History describing Severus in Aelius Spartianus

WORLD TRADE CENTRE

In the early third century some African-style ceramics appeared. York's wharves would have been the landing point for many such goods: fish and olive oil from Spain, exotic fruits from the Middle East, the finest pottery (Samian ware) from France, and wine from the Mediterranean regions were just a few of the luxuries on offer. Industries in York itself included working in metals (iron, silver, lead and copper), glass, leather, pottery and jet.

DID YOU KNOW?

Rich civilians took on priestly roles and built monuments: L Vinducius Placidus was a trader who paid for an arched gateway to a precinct (an enclosed area called a *temenos*) for a temple in York in AD221.

THE FOURTH CENTURY

A century after Severus died in York, Constantine I was declared Emperor at York in the summer of AD306, probably on the present site of York Minster. The Bishop of York, Eborius, was important enough to attend the church's Council of Arles in France in AD314, and impressive reinforcements (such as the Multangular Tower) would be added to the legionary defences.

DID YOU KNOW?

The modern statue of Constantine in York bears the inscription *hoc signo vinces* (you will conquer in this sign), recalling his vision at the battle of Milvian Bridge of a cross which prompted his conversion to Christianity.

COLLAPSE

Industry, even pottery skills, seem to have been lost in just a few decades after the Romans left in AD410. The huge Alice Holt pottery site was simply abandoned, presumably because the economic, social and political system that kept the vibrant trade alive had collapsed. Large masonry works took longer to collapse: the headquarters of the fortress may have remained standing – although used for agricultural purposes – until the ninth century.

IF YOU LIKED THIS...

Visit the Roman gallery in the Yorkshire Museum, the modern statue of Constantine and the Roman column in Deangate by the south of the Minster. You can also visit the bath-house in the Roman Baths Public House and the Multangular Tower in the Museum Gardens.

CIRENCESTER

LATIN NAME: *Corinium Dobunnorum*
DATE FOUNDED: Late AD70s
OTHER LOCAL ROMAN SITES: Gloucester
CURRENT STATUS: Continuous settlement since the Romans

Cirencester, the second largest town in Roman Britain, began as a *vicus* settlement beside an early fort. It became rich by embracing Roman life and culture and thrived into the fifth century.

BENEFITS OF ROMANISATION

The fort was built close to a native hill fort during the Claudian invasion (see p.16) in the mid-AD40s. By AD50 it had been replaced by another fort that was occupied until the AD70s. A native *vicus* settlement grew outside it and when the army moved on the economic and social life continued. The settlement was soon granted *civitas* status and the forum and basilica were built by the end of the first century, as was the amphitheatre.

RESTRICTED ACCESS

Town walls surrounded only part of the grid-patterned 107 ha (264 acres) and by the second century these walls could have housed up to 16,000 people. However, with many areas remaining under-developed, the population was probably no more than 10,000. Many of Cirencester's Roman sites are buried beneath later historical buildings, so excavations are limited.

A RICH SITE

Late second century mosaics here are among the most accomplished work in Roman Britain. This very wealthy town and its many nearby rich villas benefited from its easy access to the network of Roman roads in southern England. Unlike other towns, Cirencester's basilica remained in use throughout the fourth century.

A reconstruction of the Cirencester amphitheatre

IF YOU LIKED THIS...
Visit the Corinium Museum in Cirencester and see the riches of the Roman town, including the late fourth century mosaic of a hare set into geometric bordering patterns.

WROXETER

LATIN NAME: *Virconium Cornoviorum*
DATE FOUNDED: AD80
OTHER LOCAL ROMAN SITES: Chester
CURRENT STATUS: Roman site abandoned in the fifth or sixth century

Wroxeter began as a fort. Sited on the Roman road now called Watling Street, it became the fourth largest city in Roman Britain and contains one of the largest standing remains of a Roman building in Britain.

FROM SMALL BEGINNINGS

In c.AD58 a legionary fort replaced a mid-AD40s auxiliary fort. The army left in the late AD80s but veterans stayed on in this remote but large *civitas* capital. Native roundhouses continued to be used nearby but very few villas were built in the area.

BATHS AND BASILICAS

A forum (dedicated to Hadrian in c.AD129/AD130) was, rather inefficiently, built on top of some half-finished baths, but it was burnt down in c.AD165–AD185 and then rebuilt.

A new set of baths contained the unusual feature of a swimming pool in the courtyard outside. The *palaestra* (exercise area) was unconventional in that it had a roof but at 73m × 19.8m (240 × 65 ft) it would have been an impressive building. The vast doorway (now called the 'Old Work') to the baths is one of the largest standing remains of a Roman building.

THE ONGOING STORY

The forum was destroyed by the fourth century but commerce continued on in the now ruined baths site.

DID YOU KNOW?

The site was first excavated in 1839 and crowds flocked to view the work. Charles Dickens was one of the fascinated visitors.

Wroxeter is now a great site to visit; it is dominated by the huge section of *palaestra* wall and yet is still surrounded by fields.

A view across the ruins of the Roman baths at Wroxeter

LEICESTER

LATIN NAME: *Ratae Corieltauvorum*
DATE FOUNDED: Late first century AD
OTHER LOCAL ROMAN SITES: The Roman road, the Fosse Way
CURRENT STATUS: Modern town

Leicester (as the name *Ratae Corieltauvorum* suggests) was the 'ramparted' (*ratae*) 'administrative capital' of the Corieltauvi tribe of the East Midlands.

A GOOD SITE

Leicester fort was built in AD48 on the rising ground above the River Leir and was strategically sited to use links with Lincoln's legionary fortress (and later *colonia*). In the late first century, Leicester became the Corieltauvi's administrative centre while a Romano-British occupation at Old Sleaford, to the east, faded away.

A TRULY ROMAN TOWN

Leicester's settlement flourished and adopted grid-patterned streets and an open space for the forum. However, the

forum remained unbuilt until Hadrian's reign in the early second century. By the third century a *macellum* (covered market) as large as the forum itself, was operating.

This Romanised town had stone houses with tiled roofs, several temples, including a Mithraeum (a temple dedicated to Mithras, see p.71) and drains serving the town.

THE JEWRY WALL

The greatest survivors here are the public baths. As at Wroxeter (see p.47), the *palaestra* was a roofed hall. Equally unconventional, the *palaestra* was in a separate wing from the baths and they were connected by rooms and corridors. The still-standing wall, now called the Jewry Wall, was originally part of these second century baths. It survived by being incorporated into a Saxon church.

 IF YOU LIKED THIS...
Visit the Jewry Wall Museum to learn about the latest discoveries and to see detailed mosaics, painted wall plaster and a cavalry helmet cheek piece.

The Jewry Wall

LINCOLN

LATIN NAME: *Lindum* | DATE FOUNDED: Late AD80s/early AD90s
OTHER LOCAL ROMAN SITES: The line of the Roman road, Ermine
Street, heads north and south out of Lincoln, often along modern roads
CURRENT STATUS: Continuous settlements since the Romans

Lincoln (a shortening of *lindum colonia*) began as a legionary fortress in the AD60s, became a civilian *colonia* town in the early AD80s and was raised to provincial capital in the fourth century.

FROM FORT TO FORTIFIED TOWN

Lincoln was a hilltop Roman fortress for over 20 years before the army left, when it became a *colonia*. The old fortress walls were maintained and added to – lessons had been learnt after Colchester, which had over-confidently knocked down her walls and was then attacked by rebels in AD60 (see p.35).

A Roman arched gateway in Lincoln that is still in use

DID YOU KNOW?
Inscriptions found in Lincoln show that soldiers stationed in Lincoln came from all over the Empire, including Heraclea in Southern Italy, Lyons in France, and from Spain, Greece and Western Hungary.

In the second and third centuries, the fort's headquarters were replaced with a basilica-forum complex worthy of a town. Its rear wall (now called the Mint Wall) still stands. Masonry fragments of classical temples have also been found – a rare thing in Romano-British towns.

EXPANSION
In *c.*AD200 the local *vicus* that had built up downhill from the original fort was enclosed with the *colonia*. The *colonia* had four gates: its north gate (built in the third century) is now Newport Arch: it is the only Roman gate in Britain that traffic still passes through.

FOURTH CENTURY CHANGES
Lincoln became the capital of *Flavia Caesariensis*, one of the four provinces that Britain was split into by the early fourth century. As the road system crumbled, the town spilled outwards and spread to the River Witham.

DOVER

LATIN NAME: *Dubris*
DATE FOUNDED: c.AD85
OTHER LOCAL ROMAN SITES: Canterbury town; Rochester fort
CURRENT STATUS: Modern town

Julius Caesar's 54BC landing site became a thriving Roman town beside a fort housing the *Classis Britannica* (British Fleet). The remains of a remarkable painted house and a Roman lighthouse still stand.

THE BRITISH FLEET

Julius Caesar landed at Dover in August in 54BC but a fort was not built here until c.AD85 when the *Classis Britannica* moved from Richborough. A successful trading town soon developed next to the fort.

THE LIGHTHOUSE

The Romans enclosed Dover's large harbour with two lighthouses, one of which (the *pharos*) still stands. The first (now lost) may have been built in the first century but the lower sections of this later lighthouse have survived and contain re-used roof tiles stamped *Classis Britannica*, dating it to the early fourth century.

The remarkable design is octagonal on the outside and rectangular on the inside. Each of its four (of eight) surviving storeys is 30cm (1 ft) smaller than the one below, so the lighthouse narrows as it rises. At 13m (430 ft) it is the tallest Roman structure in Britain and probably survived because it was used as a bell tower for the medieval church beside it.

THE ROMAN PAINTED HOUSE

The Roman Painted House is the modern name for a Roman site with surviving richly-painted wall plaster. It was a *mansio* (lodge) and administrative centre in c.AD200 but, in the AD270s, it was largely demolished and incorporated into the 10 ft thick walls of the Saxon Shore Fort.

'The route from Londinium (London) to the port of Dubris (Dover) [is] 66,000 paces.'
Roman Antonine Itinerary, Iter III

This lighthouse is the tallest remaining Roman structure in Britain

GLOUCESTER

LATIN NAME: *Glevum*
DATE FOUNDED: Late first century
OTHER LOCAL ROMAN SITES: Cirencester; Caerwent
CURRENT STATUS: Modern town

Gloucester began as a fort. Even when it was a veterans' *colonia* town, it stayed within its limits, squeezing industry and fine houses within its walls which it reinforced at regular intervals.

A SOLDIERS' HOME

In AD64–AD66, a legionary fort was built 400m south of an earlier (c.AD49) fort at Kingsholm. The army left the fort at the end of the century and the veterans stayed in this *colonia* settlement. Instead of taking good land from the locals they drained the nearby River Severn's flood plain for farmland.

WITHIN THESE WALLS

The fort walls at Gloucester were preserved and the settlement was tightly packed inside its 19 hectares (46 acres). Iron-smithing and pottery-firing took place in the old barrack blocks, while the first forum and basilica were built using timber and gravel on the site of the demolished *principia* (fort headquarters).

A port did eventually get built but Gloucester never became a market centre: as the area became more settled, Caerwent and Cirencester grew into flourishing economic competition. Nonetheless, the town was improved in the second century and mosaic floors appeared in some houses.

DID YOU KNOW?

A modern statue of Nerva on horseback commemorates the date of Gloucester's founding. It stands at the entrance to Gloucester's Eastgate Shopping Centre, on the site where fragments of a Roman bronze equestrian statue were found.

THE END IN SIGHT

At the end of the century, rectangular towers were added to the town walls, and a century later, the walls were strengthened and external towers added to the four gates. However, these did not stop the Saxons: after they won a battle at Dyrham in AD577, they seized Gloucester, Cirencester and Bath. Roman Britain had ended.

A statue of the Emperor Nerva in Gloucester

Forts, Villas and Sites

Rome introduced more than just towns into Britain: after the invasion forts, villas and public buildings began to spread across the land. The ruins of military posts, opulent villas, baths and amphitheatres are some of the most dramatic reminders of Roman Britain.

FORTS

The first structures to appear were the military forts that housed the soldiers and secured the land. Built first of timber and earthen ramparts with a gate in each side, their construction was an efficient and fast process – every soldier knew his role.

A grid-pattern of barracks and granaries surrounded the central headquarters (*principia*) with its open area and sunken secure vault for the soldiers' pay and adjacent commandant's multi-roomed house (*praetorium*).

Over time, defensive stone walls would usually be erected and baths built outside them. Local circumstances and requirements led to some variations, and samples of these adaptations (such as Ardoch's defensive ditches, see p.54) are found throughout Britain.

VILLAS

However, by the time the Antonine Wall was being built in the AD140s (see p.25), other military building was slowing down, as were public building works in towns. After the late first century, resources were increasingly invested in another type of building – the villas.

Britain had been filled with farms since before the Romans arrived, but now some became new 'estate' farms, centred around a gradually improved stone residence that included bath houses, painted plaster walls and hypocausts for underfloor heating beneath mosaic floors. See p.62 for more on how their designs became more luxurious.

OTHER SITES

While forts and villas are among the most visible of Roman remains in Britain, other

LOCATIONS

1. **Ardoch**
Alauna veniconum

2. **Corbridge**
Corstopium/Coriosopitum

3. **Hadrian's Wall**
Vallum Aelium

4. **Housesteads Fort**
Vercovicium

5. **Arbeia**
Arbeia

6. **Vindolanda**
Vindolanda

7. **Richborough**
Rutupiae

8. **Fishbourne Palace**
(Latin name unknown)

9. **Brading Villa**
(Latin name unknown)

10. **Chedworth Villa**
(Latin name unknown)

11. **Lullingstone Villa**
(Latin name unknown)

12. **Chester Amphitheatre**
Deva

13. **Bearsden Bath House**
(Latin name unknown)

major structures are well worth noting.

A crucial element of Roman towns was their monumental public buildings. These included amphitheatres, where gladiator games and animal baiting were watched by thousands of spectators. Despite their grand scale, many amphitheatres are now lost (buried or demolished over time) but remains of such sites can still be seen at London, Caerleon and Chester. It was only in 2010 that archaeological surveyors discovered an amphitheatre at Aldborough in Yorkshire.

A ubiquitous Roman structure was the bath house, like the one at Bearsden (see p.69). A vital part of Roman life, these were used daily and were built at towns, forts and the grander villas.

A complete complex consisted of a changing room (*apodyterium*), an exercise yard (*palaestra*), a cold room (*frigidarium*) with a cold plunge bath, a warm room (*tepidarium*) and a hot steam room with a plunge bath (a hot tub, in effect).

ARDOCH

LATIN NAME: *Alauna Veniconum* | **LOCATION:** Perthshire/Tayside
DATE FOUNDED: c.AD80
OTHER LOCAL ROMAN SITES: Small forts at Glenbank and Cairns Castle
CURRENT STATUS: Open to visitors

Vast earthworks dominate Ardoch fort: built in c.AD80 during the first Roman advance into Scotland, it became one of a series of Roman forts built along the Gask ridge between Dunblane and Perth.

A MILITARY PRESENCE IN THE NORTH

A view of the striking ditches of Ardoch

Although the south of England was quickly pacified and forts soon became residential *colonia*, things were different in the north: Agricola's push north (see p.75) created a permanent military zone in northern England and in Scotland for a time.

ON CAMPAIGN

Ardoch was built during this first Roman advance north, leading up to the decisive Roman victory at *Mons Graupius* somewhere in east Scotland in AD83. Ardoch now has few signs of any buildings within the fort – only the *principia* (headquarters) in the centre of the fort. However, the earthworks are most impressive (still 2m deep with five ditches surviving in places). They are evidence of the active campaign being fought at the time.

A SECOND CAMPAIGN

Although the fort was abandoned in c.AD86/7 when the Roman army was withdrawn from Scotland, Ardoch was re-occupied and enlarged during Emperor Antonius Pius' advance in the AD140s when the Antonine wall was built (see p.25). A regiment of between 500 and 1,000 Spanish auxiliaries were stationed at this strategic site making it one of the largest Roman stations in Britain. Within 20 years though, the Romans left Scotland for good and the site was abandoned.

ARDOCH TODAY

Ardoch is an atmospheric site to visit, with its dramatic deep ditches. Open at all times to walkers, it is a large and abrupt feature in the landscape.

IF YOU LIKED THIS...

Look out for the Roman signal station, built over by the second fort's eastern defences: a square enclosure c.11sqm (36 sq. ft.) surrounded by a 3m (10 ft) ditch and bank, it sits beside the old Roman road.

CORBRIDGE

LATIN NAME: *Corstopitum/Coriosopitum* **but locally called** *Coria*
LOCATION: Northumberland | **DATE FOUNDED:** c.AD86
OTHER LOCAL ROMAN SITES: Stanegate Road; Dere Street;
Brunton Turret

Built in c.AD86, Corbridge was just south of Hadrian's Wall where Dere Street (the main north road) met Stanegate Road (the east to west military road). Its changing fortunes reflect those of Roman forts.

TIMBER FORTS

During Agricola's campaign northwards, Corbridge fort was built to guard the crossing at the River Tyne. Like many forts in the north, it was first built in turf and timber, but in AD103 it was deliberately burnt down to allow a new fort with stone headquarters (*principia*) and commandant's house (*praetorium*) to be built.

DID YOU KNOW?

An early fort, complete with a bath house, had been built in c.AD79. Although excavated in the 1950s and given an Emergency Preservation Order, the site was later damaged.

EVER-CHANGING FORTS

The Romans adapted forts as necessary and Corbridge was rebuilt several times as its role changed with the advance and retreat of the Romans' northern frontier. It was strengthened in AD122 to support the building of Hadrian's Wall, but forts were needed on the Wall itself and Corbridge (being a short distance from the Wall) became nothing more than a civilian town.

Corbridge proved a versatile fort as it was rebuilt several times

As Corbridge was on the main route north, it was refurbished in stone in AD410 as it was essential again as Rome's 'front line' moved north to the Antonine Wall.

A SOLID CENTRE

By the third century, a sprawling, thriving walled town had built up around the fort. When the Romans left, the Saxons used its ruined buildings – a valuable resource in a time largely devoid of any new stone building work – before abandoning the site entirely.

CORBRIDGE TODAY

Nowadays Corbridge is a well-excavated site where you can explore the ruins of buildings and see the artefacts (including weapons and armour) found here in the site museum.

HADRIAN'S WALL

LATIN NAME: *Vallum Aelium*

LOCATION: Across Northern England from the Solway to the Tyne

DATE FOUNDED: Work began in AD122

OTHER LOCAL ROMAN SITES: Forts, milecastles and watchtowers

Hadrian's Wall was built under governor Nepos' command, on the orders of Emperor Hadrian (AD117–AD138) after his visit to Britain in AD119. The Wall ran 117km (73 miles) from the Solway to the Tyne.

WHAT WAS THE WALL FOR?

The Wall established a frontier line that Emperor Trajan (AD98–AD117) had drawn up. Hadrian's biographer claimed the purpose of the Wall was to 'divide' the Romans and barbarians, but in reality it was a fortified, gated barrier to hold back raiders and control movement.

DID YOU KNOW?

The Romans called the Wall, *Vallum Aelium* **in honour of Hadrian's full name:** *Publius Aelius Hadrianus*.

GRAND DESIGNS

The original orders for the Wall stated it should be 10 Roman feet (3m) wide and at least 15 Roman feet (4.5m) high, built 20 Roman feet (5.9m) behind a forward ditch. A Roman foot was half an inch shorter than a modern foot. There was to be a fortified gateway/milecastle with accommodation for around 12 soldiers every Roman mile, linked by two watchtowers at a third of a mile intervals.

However, money, resources or time reduced the Wall, even while it was being built, to 8 ft in width and the ditch was abandoned where the rock was too hard to cut. Forts, like Housesteads, were built right onto the wall.

Once the forts were built, a huge 5.9m (20 ft) wide *vallum* (flat bottomed ditch)

Much of Hadrian's Wall can still be followed on foot

was dug parallel to the south of the wall to create a protected military zone.

DID YOU KNOW?

An estimated 3.7 million tonnes of local sandstone were used to build Hadrian's Wall. It took two thirds of Britain's support troops to man it.

HOW WAS IT BUILT?

The Wall took members from all three of Britain's legions (*II Augusta*, *VI Victrix* and *XX Valeria Victrix*) and members of the fleet (*Classis Britannica*) to build. However, the wall was simply roughly-dressed stone filled with rubble held together with lime mortar: it was quick to build but frost and erosion soon took their toll.

IF YOU LIKED THIS...

Visit Birdoswald fort in Cumbria, where the Wall construction is visible. The double-entrance at the east gate is the best preserved fort gate in Britain.

A FAVOURED FRONTIER

The Wall was abandoned in favour of the new Antonine Wall in AD142 (see p.25) but within 20 years the Romans retreated back to Hadrian's Wall. Later in the second century some turrets were taken out of service and some milecastles were blocked up.

WEIRD AND WONDERFUL

Milecastles were built with gates in the Wall, even when there was an almost vertical cliff on the barbarian side (as at Milecastle 39).

Milecastle 39 still looks impressive

ATTACK FROM THE NORTH

The Wall was not invincible: when Clodius Albinus took much of Britain's troops to Gaul in the AD190s to support his claim as Emperor, tribes from Scotland ravaged the Wall (see p.25) as they invaded down to fortresses as far south as York and Chester. Once order was restored, a vast rebuilding plan was carried out from AD197–AD208.

When the Picts and Scots raided south during the 'barbarian conspiracy' of AD367, workers were sent from the *civitas* capitals to restore the Wall. However, by the end of the fourth century, much of the Wall had fallen into disrepair.

THE WALL TODAY

It is possible to walk most of the length of the Wall but in some areas it has eroded away and in the past it was robbed for building material. The most dramatic section is along the high escarpments close to Housesteads Fort.

HOUSESTEADS FORT

LATIN NAME: *Vercovicium*
LOCATION: Northumberland
DATE FOUNDED: c.AD122
OTHER LOCAL ROMAN SITES: Vindolanda; The Roman Army Museum

Housesteads was built in c.AD122 as one of the forts on Hadrian's Wall. With its dramatic cliff-top location, it is one of the most complete remains of a fort on Hadrian's Wall.

WHAT'S AT HOUSESTEADS?

Although first built in c.AD128, Housesteads' visible remains mostly date to the third and fourth century. They include outer walls and stone gateways that still stand at a good height, regimented barrack blocks, the *principia* and *praetorium*, the substantial granaries, extremely well-preserved latrines, as well as a rare fort hospital.

A NATURAL INCLINE

Forts were usually built on a north to south axis but Housesteads was built east to west. This was because the fort had to be built against Hadrian's Wall, which formed the fort's north wall. The landscape here meant the fort was located on a steep incline: its name, *Vercovicium*, means the 'town on the slope'.

 DID YOU KNOW?
The houses in the *vicus* line, the road that ran south from the fort, headed straight down the steep hill, not along the modern, less strenuous route.

THE LATER FORT

Major building works (c.AD198, AD296 and AD367) adapted the fort for the different legions and auxiliary troops were stationed here through the centuries. In the late fourth century, barbarian attacks caused civilians from the *vicus* to move into, and re-design, the fort.

HOUSESTEADS TODAY

Today, Housesteads is one of the most impressive forts along Hadrian's Wall: walls, pavings and the latrines are supplemented by extensive views and an on-site museum.

The remains of Housesteads Fort still impress

ARBEIA

LATIN NAME: *Arbeia*

LOCATION: South Shields, Tyne and Wear

DATE FOUNDED: c.AD129

OTHER LOCAL ROMAN SITES: *Pons Aelius* (Newcastle)

Arbeia, at the eastern end of Hadrian's Wall, was a major coastal fort on the south bank of the River Tyne. Its fortunes follow those of the Roman campaigns on this frontier line and into Scotland.

Arbeia's ruins are now part of an impressive recreated guesthouse and museum

BUILT FOR A PURPOSE

Arbeia Fort was originally purpose-built in c.AD129 as the easternmost point on Hadrian's Wall. It guarded a small port on the Tyne Estuary and so provided safe access to and from the North Sea. Support cavalry troops were stationed here and a large cobbled parade ground was found, but the stone fort visible today dates to c.AD160.

BREAD BASKET OF THE NORTH

Severus' campaigns into Scotland began in AD208, prompting the fort to adopt a new role. It was redesigned to house infantry rather than cavalry, and extended to accommodate 18 stone granaries as the supply base for the campaigns.

GRAND DESIGNS

The fort fell from use for much of the third century (while most of the Roman army was away fighting in Europe, see p.28). By the early fourth century, most forts were in decay but, in c.AD300, Arbeia burnt down and was rebuilt yet again. Several buildings were re-located within the fort and the commandant's house was redesigned, rather strangely, as a comfortable Mediterranean courtyard-style villa.

WEIRD AND WONDERFUL

Inside the *praetorium*, the dining room was laid out in grand Roman style with couches to lie on, but a later, smaller dining room – heated by hypocaust system – was added for use in the cold winter months.

When the Roman army left Britain in AD410, Arbeia was abandoned for ever.

ARBEIA TODAY

Visitors can explore the excavated ruins, an impressive reconstructed gateway, barracks and *praetorium* and its on-site museum.

VINDOLANDA

LATIN NAME: *Vindolanda* | **LOCATION:** Bardon Mill, Northumberland
DATE FOUNDED: c.AD85 (pre-Hadrian's Wall)
OTHER LOCAL ROMAN SITES: Housesteads Fort; Mithraeum
at *Brocolitia*

Vindolanda lies just south of Hadrian's Wall and is a fascinating site where leather shoes and priceless wooden writing tablets have survived to give us a unique insight into life on the Roman frontier.

MILITARY DEFENCE

A timber fort was built here in c.AD85 as part of the frontier along the Stanegate road during Domitian's retreat from Scotland. Auxiliary cohorts were stationed here almost continuously until the Romans left Britain in AD410. In that time, they rebuilt the fort at least six times but only the last two forts were stone forts. The first was built in Hadrian's time and it is the last fort, dating from AD212, with its walls, granaries, headquarters, commandant's house, paved roadway and external bathhouses and once-vibrant civilian *vicus*, that you can visit today.

DID YOU KNOW?

The Birthday Invitation – the most famous of Vindolanda's writing tablets – contains the earliest handwriting by a Roman woman anywhere in the Empire.

ARCHAEOLOGICAL TREASURES

At Vindolanda you can walk around an archaeological site that is continually being extended and uncovered. As you visit the fort and civilian town (*vicus*) that grew up at its gates you can watch the annual summer excavations.

The finds dug up here are unique – they were sealed by clay in damp, oxygen-free conditions that enabled even organic materials like wood, leather, hair and woven basket material to survive, providing a rare glimpse into the details of Roman life.

VINDOLANDA TODAY

Managed by the Vindolanda Trust since its discovery in the 1970s, this site and its museum (renovated in 2011) are essential visits that provide an unparalleled insight into life along and near the Wall.

The Vindolanda ruins provide an exciting tourist attraction

RICHBOROUGH

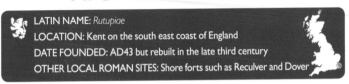

LATIN NAME: *Rutupiae*

LOCATION: Kent on the south east coast of England

DATE FOUNDED: AD43 but rebuilt in the late third century

OTHER LOCAL ROMAN SITES: Shore forts such as Reculver and Dover

After the northern military renovations, new forts – the Saxon Shore Forts – were built on the coast of southern England in the third century and early AD300s as a defence against raiders.

THE LAUNCH OF ROMAN BRITAIN

The first fort here had been built in Claudius' invasion back in AD43 and the Roman road, Watling Street, headed out of its West Gate to take troops to Canterbury and on to London. A monumental marble-clad arch was built here in Domitian's rule (AD81–AD96) to commemorate the conquest (only its base survives now). The fort remained a main port of entry for Rome into Britain in the first and second centuries and, like so many forts, sheltered a Romanised civilian settlement.

WEIRD AND WONDERFUL

Archaeologists have found parts of the Roman harbour wall and even the ancient beach here but the surprise is that the Roman shoreline was two miles further inland than today's coastline.

THE MIGHT OF ROMAN BRITAIN

The late third century fort is much smaller but it was very solidly built: although most buildings inside the fort were timber, huge 3.3m (11 ft) thick stone outer walls mark this last phase of Roman fort building in Britain: parts of the walls still stand to 8m (25 ft) in height.

THE LAST STAND FOR ROMAN BRITAIN

A large number of Roman coins dated AD395–AD402 were found at Richborough: few Roman coins dating from after AD379 are found in Britain, so this could be a rare and final image of the Roman army's pay in Britain. Richborough had seen the start of Rome's military bases in Britain: now, nearly 400 years later, it was one of the last.

A stunning image of Richborough's triple ditches

ROMAN VILLAS

Villas were a very Roman concept. They were essentially farms – rural estates with outbuildings – but they increasingly displayed the growing wealth of their inhabitants in showy architectural extensions, mosaics, wall paintings and private bath houses.

EARLY VILLAS

Many villas had humble beginnings. First century villas were little more than simple farms set on good farming land with access to a spring or fresh water river.

Outbuildings like barns and a smithy (where iron was worked) were common but the Roman habit of social climbing was soon felt in the south and the Midlands. Locals wanted to impress both the powerful newcomers and neighbours alike. They also wanted to take advantage of the increased economic opportunities and luxuries the Romans provided. By the end of the first century, new multi-roomed, rectangular farmhouses boasting Roman luxury goods acted as highly visible status symbols.

DID YOU KNOW?

In the second century Younger Pliny wrote that a man of his status should have a house of architectural features, dining rooms, libraries, baths, bedrooms and colonnades.

WHO LIVED IN VILLAS?

We don't know the name of any villa owner in Britain, however, Romano-British villas reveal the owners' desires to be considered 'Roman'. Country villas were seen as echoes of Rome's mythical rural origins and its rise to greatness, and they displayed an obvious pleasure in Roman culture in features like sophisticated architecture blended with mosaics that portrayed Roman deities and mythical figures.

DID YOU KNOW?

The mosaics in a villa might reflect the owner's personality: the astronomer or philosopher depicted in Brading Villa's mosaics would tell visitors that they were in the presence of an educated man.

THE GRANDEUR OF THIRD AND FOURTH CENTURY VILLAS

Towns began to deteriorate in the third century and money once spent on public

Great Witcombe was originally a luxurious hillside villa

Mosaics were used not just as a sign of wealth but also character

buildings was now spent on showy improvements to villas. First extended into two-winged buildings and then, in the fourth century, into 'courtyard villas' with wings on every side, they were grander than ever before and screamed status and personal wealth. Now villas boasted colonnades, statues and garden landscaping and were decorated by craftsmen, often using foreign imported materials.

WHAT HAPPENED AFTER THE ROMANS LEFT?

From the AD380s villas were in decline: the Roman economy that they depended on was losing its grip. New building stopped and repairs were botched. After the Romans left in AD410, money wasn't available, new materials were no longer accessible and the skills were forgotten. Although the decline was gradual and some villas continued to be lived in after AD410, they eventually fell into disrepair and became little more than shelters as fires were lit on the mosaic floors.

'The Britons were led into a taste for those tempting luxuries: porticos and baths and fine dining, and, unsuspecting, they called it politeness, while in reality, they were an aspect of their slavery.'
Tacitus, Roman historian, Agricola 21

VISITING ROMAN VILLAS IN BRITAIN

Most Roman villas in Britain were built in the south and Midlands – few can be found in the north or in Wales. They range from the earliest (Fishbourne, see p.64) through every era to the final decades of the Roman period and beyond (as at Lullingstone, see p.67). Look out for mosaic floors, hypocaust systems and dining rooms, as well as extensions and special individual features such as shrines or Lullingstone's church room.

IF YOU LIKED THIS...
As well as those listed in this book, try visiting Bignor Villa (West Sussex), famous for its mosaics, and Littlecote Villa (Berkshire) with its restored mosaic. If you're in Gloucestershire, see the elaborate baths at Great Witcombe hillside winged villa. A rare northern villa is Beadlam's winged-corridor villa, in Helmsley, North Yorkshire.

FISHBOURNE PALACE

LATIN NAME: Unknown
LOCATION: Chichester
DATE FOUNDED: AD70
OTHER LOCAL ROMAN SITES: Chichester; Bignor Roman Villa

Villas are the great indicator of the acceptance of Roman culture in Britain. The earliest Roman villa we know of is Fishbourne and it was a villa fit for a king.

THE FIRST HINT OF ROME

Fishbourne Palace was discovered and excavated in the 1960s. Signs of very early Roman trading (imperial pottery and Roman scabbard fittings) were found in the Iron Age levels, quickly followed by a couple of Roman military-type buildings dating from the mid-AD40s. This shows that Romans had settled here quickly after Claudius' invasion in AD43.

ROMAN INFLUENCES

Within five years, these military buildings were replaced by a timber house that was decorated with painted plaster walls – a

Fishbourne's extensive mosaics are a sign of its very Roman grandeur

sure sign of Romanisation. By the AD60s, a new stone house had been built. It was equipped with baths, mosaics and marble paving. This was revolutionary and very Roman, and only a local chief could have afforded such a building. By AD80 a new palace replaced even this splendour: sprawling over 4 hectares (10 acres) the villa had four wings that enclosed formal landscaped gardens.

WHO LIVED HERE?

It is possible that Fishbourne was the palace of Tiberius Claudius Togidubnus, a local tribal King praised by Roman historian, Tacitus, for his loyalty to Rome.

FISHBOURNE TODAY

The site has been extensively excavated since its discovery and there are many rooms and mosaics as well as a reconstructed Roman garden to explore here.

IF YOU LIKED THIS...

Visit nearby Bignor to view the stunning mosaics and to see how the local mosaics developed in the third century.

BRADING VILLA

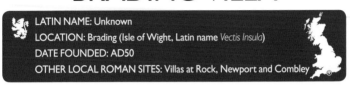

LATIN NAME: Unknown
LOCATION: Brading (Isle of Wight, Latin name *Vectis Insula*)
DATE FOUNDED: AD50
OTHER LOCAL ROMAN SITES: Villas at Rock, Newport and Combley

Southern farms, already familiar with Roman goods, quickly adopted Roman culture. At Brading, an Iron Age roundhouse was replaced as early as AD50 by a Romano-British rectangular timber house.

THE ROMANS ARRIVE

Excavations at Brading Villa found evidence of rich hunting and plentiful local seafood, crops and sheep, as well as sea-borne trade

Roman treasures like this continue to be discovered at Brading villa

from Europe. This rich location was soon filled with Roman luxuries and craftsmen: traditional roundhouses were replaced by timber rectangular crofts and these, in their turn, were rebuilt in stone.

ROMAN LUXURY

Like most villas, Brading villa was gradually extended and enhanced. By the middle of the second century, it had built up into three wings around a garden and included bath suites. Inside, the walls were decorated with plaster, brightly painted with woodland and floral scenes. Luxuries such as Samian ware pottery from France, olive oil and wine from Greece and Italy, and quality quern stones (for grinding flour) from Germany had all reached the farm. It was a working estate as well, with workshops, storage buildings and a granary.

FULL CIRCLE

Most villas in southern England were at their grandest in the third century but Brading was devastated by fire. Although the estate continued to be farmed, its glory days were over: the fine rooms were used for agricultural storage and the building fell into decay after AD395.

DID YOU KNOW?

Brading villa was found in 1879 by Mr Munns, a local farmer, and Captain Thorp when an iron bar used to make holes for a sheep pen struck a mosaic floor. They set to work to uncover more and excavations continue to explore the site today.

BRADING VILLA TODAY

Today Brading villa benefits from an impressive all-weather modern award-winning exhibition and visitor centre built by the independent charity which runs the site.

Forts, Villas and Sites

CHEDWORTH VILLA

LATIN NAME: Unknown
LOCATION: Chedworth, near Cheltenham, Gloucestershire
DATE FOUNDED: by AD150
OTHER LOCAL ROMAN SITES: Great Witcombe villa

Chedworth villa is one of the largest villas in Britain and includes fine mosaics, bath houses, hypocausts, latrines and a water-shrine.

The mosaics at Chedworth are some of the finest designs to be discovered

HUMBLE ORIGINS

Chedworth began as a plain, inexpensive Roman house, built close to a natural spring but by AD150 the villa was already remarkable for its size. Sometime later, fire damage was immediately repaired and the site was enlarged to include a bath house.

RELIGIOUS CENTRE

A stone altar stood beside a humble and ancient water-shrine centred on a spring that provided water for the site. Remains of the Roman household gods (see p.70) were found here, as well as an impressively-colonnaded square temple dating from the second century that was located at the nearby River Coln.

DID YOU KNOW?

A stone found in the water shrine here was inscribed with the Christian Chi-Rho sign: Christian and pagan religion typically rubbed shoulders in Roman Britain.

FOURTH CENTURY REGAL GRANDEUR

Fortunes were spent on villas in the fourth century and Chedworth was no exception. This grand hillside villa contained over 50 rooms in long wings, linked by a colonnaded corridor around an open area. Over 100 people lived and worked here. Its size and the fine mosaic floors, quantities of costly imported wine and olive oil in amphorae, and hypocaust systems in nearly every room indicate that this house belonged to a rich and powerful owner. A large dining suite and a grand bath complex were added by the late fourth century.

Nonetheless, within a couple of decades of the Romans leaving Britain in AD410, the villa fell into decay.

CHEDWORTH TODAY

Chedworth villa site was redeveloped during 2011, making the extensive ruins and excellent mosaics an even greater experience for visitors.

LULLINGSTONE VILLA

LATIN NAME: Unknown
LOCATION: Lullingstone, near Eynsford, Kent
DATE FOUNDED: c.AD100
OTHER LOCAL ROMAN SITES: Dover lighthouse and painted house

Lullingstone villa, like Chedworth (see p.66), included a religious element: while its mosaics have a mythical theme, its Christian paintings are unique. Lullingstone is amongst the last of the Roman villas in Britain.

AN EXTENSIVE SITE

After a humble start in c.AD100, when it was first built with wattle (timber) and daub (mud), the villa was rebuilt in stone in the second century and altered many times. It extended to an immense 24 rooms, including a bath suite, with at least four more rooms being set aside from the main building – a semi circular shrine, a kitchen, a granary and a fourth century mausoleum (later incorporated into a Saxon church).

A RICH SITE

The rare apsidal shaped (ie with a semi-circular end) dining room was added in c.AD360 and it contained mosaics decorated with geometric designs. The mosaics depicted the faces of the four seasons shown around an image of Bellerophon (a hero from Greek mythology).

WEIRD AND WONDERFUL

The image of Bellerophon killing the Chimera was sometimes used as a secret Christian symbol for God/good overcoming the devil and evil.

A UNIQUE SITE

Amongst Lullingstone's treasures are Christian wall paintings – the coded Chi-Rho symbol and Christians praying – on the walls of a cellar that served as a unique Roman house church. Unusually, the house continued to be used after the Romans left in AD410 but it was abandoned after a fire in AD420.

LULLINGSTONE TODAY

Visitors can view this large villa with its mosaics and unique church room, as well as the artefacts that were found here.

The remains of Lullingstone look captivating in this light

Forts, Villas and Sites

CHESTER AMPHITHEATRE

LATIN NAME: *Deva*
LOCATION: Chester, Cheshire
DATE FOUNDED: First century AD
OTHER LOCAL ROMAN SITES: Wroxeter town

Chester's amphitheatre is the largest in Roman Britain and could seat at least 8,000 people. It is sited within a large curving modern road system. Excavations began as recently as 2000.

To date, only half of the Chester amphitheatre has been excavated

A HIGH STATUS SITE

The legionary fortresses at Chester were built at the north and south ends of the governor Frontinus' push against the troublesome tribes in Wales in the AD70s. Agricola (see p.75) finished this work in subduing the Welsh, and Chester was established as a central administrative site as early at the AD80s.

A MONUMENTAL WORK

A simple wooden amphitheatre was built in the late AD70s, with wooden seating and a stairway on the rear wall to the upper seats. This was used until the legion left to help to build Hadrian's Wall in the AD120s but it was rebuilt in c.AD275 as a stone amphitheatre, 98m (320 ft) by 87m (286 ft), with eight vaulted stairways providing access to the upper tiers.

WHAT IS AN AMPHITHEATRE FOR?

Chester's amphitheatre hosted entertainment in the forms of gladiatorial shows, animal baiting, boxing and wrestling. Spectators could buy bowls decorated with images of gladiators as souvenirs, and refreshments were on sale.

Chester's amphitheatre, like most amphitheatres, was placed outside the city walls. Processions were made from a town's temples out to its amphitheatre as part of religious festivals and in Chester a small shrine was found by the amphitheatre's entrance.

CHESTER AMPHITHEATRE TODAY

Encircled by the modern city, the scale of the Roman amphitheatre, with its open space surrounded by banks (where the seating was), is still evident today even though only half of it has been excavated.

IF YOU LIKED THIS...
Visit Caerleon fort, at the southern end of the Roman advance into Wales. It was similarly equipped with an amphitheatre.

BEARSDEN BATH HOUSE

LATIN NAME: *Unknown*
LOCATION: Bearsden, East Dunbartonshire
DATE FOUNDED: AD140s
OTHER LOCAL ROMAN SITES: Antonine Wall

Bearsden's bath house was built as part of a fort at the time of the Antonine Wall (AD140s). It gives us a taste of Rome's influence at its furthest reach, in briefly occupied Scotland.

A BRIEF, TOUGH OCCUPATION

The fort at Bearsden was one of 16 built along the Antonine Wall in the AD140s. It was occupied for a mere 12 years before it was abandoned. The construction of the fort's bath house, even though the army was here for only a short time, reveals how essential such facilities were for the Romans.

WHAT DID THE BATH HOUSE INCLUDE?

The complex includes the all-essential changing room (*apodyterium*), the cold

room (*frigidarium*), a cold bath, two warm steam rooms (*tepidarium*), a hot steam room (*caldarium*) and hot dry room (*sudatorium*), plus a nearby latrine. The warm rooms were heated by a hypocaust system that allowed the heat from an adjacent hearth to funnel beneath the floor and up channels in the walls.

BEARSDEN BATH HOUSE TODAY

Discovered in the 1970s during building work for flats in the centre of Bearsden, this bath house is all that remains of the now lost fort. The site is remarkable for the preservation of the foundations of the buildings. The plunge bath is particularly fine.

Beasden bath house remains well preserved

IF YOU LIKED THIS...
The finds (including sculpture and inscriptions) discovered at Bearsden Bath House can be seen at the University of Glasgow's Hunterian Museum.

RELIGION UNDER THE ROMANS

In Roman religion, the gods were everywhere, and religion infiltrated every part of life. Temples were built in the towns but forts and even villas in Britain are littered with altars, shrines and inscriptions.

CELTIC RELIGION

Pre-Roman Britain was a land of spirits worshipped at sacred springs and groves. Rome normally absorbed the local religions of conquered lands into her own, identifying the local god as one of their own in a different character. For example Bath's Sulis became linked with Roman Minerva and became Sulis Minerva. This avoided local bad feeling but also Romanised religion and helped to reinforce Roman ways.

DID YOU KNOW?

When Agricola attacked and wiped out the druids on Anglesey it had little to do with religion: it was a violent political move to end their power that threatened Roman control in Britain.

DEAL OR NO DEAL

Romans believed that just about anything had a god or spirit, even door hinges! The gods were thought to be interested in humans only in a bored, playful way and a Roman's relationship with the gods had no moral aspect. Instead, it was a business transaction: a mortal promised an offering (like a temple or a sacrifice) in return for something from the god (eg victory in battle). Some temples were laden with donated votive/prayer offerings and, more negatively, curses (see p.39).

WEIRD AND WONDERFUL

The Roman description of their business approach to the gods was *manus manum lavat* or 'hand washes hand', reflecting their concept that both parties benefited from each other.

WHO DID THEY PRAY TO?

Specific gods included 'household gods' in Roman homes and temples were

The Persian god Mithras

built to the 'Pantheon' of gods (such as Jupiter, Mars, Neptune and Minerva). There was also the Imperial Cult of the divine Emperor, whose worship was a required gesture of loyalty to Rome.

Mystery cults (such as those dedicated to Isis or Cybele) involved a more personal response (sometimes even self-harm) in worship. The exotic Persian cult of Mithras (a men-only cult involving ranks and initiation ceremonies) was popular among soldiers, and it proclaimed the new idea of salvation through rebirth, all linked in with good versus evil. *Mithraea* (temples of Mithras) have been found in London and near forts, such as at Carrawburgh, Northumberland.

CHRISTIANITY

In AD312, Constantine was converted to Christianity following a vision and he made Christianity the official state religion. In AD313 the Edict of Milan guaranteed that the previously persecuted Christians would receive religious tolerance. Lullingstone villa (see p.67) provides a glimpse into a church house in Britain later that century.

WEIRD AND WONDERFUL

Christians risked persecution for their faith, and so a number of coded signals were used to display 'The Way' (as Christianity was called). Word squares and the Chi-Rho monogram sign (the first letters of Christ's name in Greek) have been found in Britain.

An uncovered mithraeum ruin

TEMPLES

Romano-Celtic temples were common in Britain. A single central *cella* (room) holding the image of the god was surrounded by a roofed concentric walkway, and several of these temples might be built within a *temenos* (walled enclosure). Classical temples with steps up to a pedimented *cella* were much rarer in Britain, even though the huge temple to the deified Claudius was built at Colchester soon after the invasion in AD43. At temples, officials would take on priestly roles, make sacrifices of live animals and read the *auspices* (messages from the gods) in their entrails.

DID YOU KNOW?

Geographical places appeared on Roman coins, often as women, personifying the country that had been conquered. *Britannia* made her first appearance in AD119 on a coin of the Emperor Hadrian and by AD142 she is found in her traditional pose, seated on a rock, with a shield beside her.

Roman Governors

The Roman province of Britain was run by the governor, a personal representative of the Emperor. Based in London and later in York, Lincoln and Cirencester it was a demanding but powerful posting that was rich with potential.

WHAT DID A GOVERNOR DO?

Called a *legatus* (Legate), or *propraetor*, the governor was in full command of both military and civilian affairs in the province. Nonetheless, he was appointed by the Emperor and answered directly to him.

Only those who had worked up the strict Roman hierarchical political career ladder and who qualified as senatorial class (by owning property worth one million *sesterces*) were eligible for this prestigious post. No Britons ever qualified in this way: to the Romans, Britain always remained a land of barbarians that needed ruling.

In the fourth century, Britain was divided into four provinces ruled from London, Cirencester, York and Lincoln, and control of civil administration was separated from military command, meaning the governor was now responsible for civilian matters only.

JOB PROSPECTS

There was no set period for a governor's term of office but, with a few exceptions, two to four years was usual and it was a valued stepping stone to governorships in richer provinces such as Syria.

Because Britain remained unsettled in the north, it was a highly demanding military posting. By the end of the first century AD, an imperial judicial Legate was introduced as a deputy to ease the load. This was an ideal promotion for a Legionary Legate (an officer in charge of a legion) who hoped to go on to be a governor in another province.

Rome habitually employed 'client kings' (such as Prasutagus, Boudicca's husband),

The governor of Britain was in command of military affairs

existing rulers who remained only as a puppet ruler, loyal to the governor of Rome and to the Emperor.

The Imperial Procurator was the most senior administrative post in Britain. Based in London (like the governor), he was fully responsible for the province's finances. However, extortion by the governor to line his own pockets, or by his bureaucratic officials, was always a possibility.

A POWERFUL POST

As the Emperor's personal delegate, the governor deferred to any Emperor who visited Britain. These included Claudius in his fortnight's triumphal visit in AD43, Hadrian on his tour in AD119 preceding his order to build the Wall, Severus in his inconclusive campaign into Scotland in AD208–AD211, and Constantine after his proclamation as Emperor in York in AD306.

REBEL GOVERNORS

Rebel governors like Clodius Albinus (AD195–AD197) occasionally challenged imperial power and Britain was part of the breakaway Gallic Empire of Postumus from AD260–AD269. Carausius, the

commander of the British fleet, ruled the province from AD 286–AD293. All usurpers of power were ultimately killed except Constantine who went on to become Emperor in AD324.

A statue of governor Agricola at Bath

PLAUTIUS

FULL NAME: Aulus Plautius | DATE OF GOVERNORSHIP: AD43–AD46
EMPEROR DURING GOVERNORSHIP: Claudius (AD41–AD54)
RELATED SITES: All early invasion sites in southern, western and central
England, especially Richborough, Fishbourne and Colchester

The Roman historian, Tacitus, recorded that 'the first consular governor to be placed in command of Britain was Aulus Plautius'. He was also the general who led Rome to her first true conquest of Britain.

THE RIGHT MAN FOR THE JOB

Plautius had solid political and military experience. He had held the highest political rank (just below the Emperor) as consul in Rome and had governed Pannonia (a territory on the Danube). He also had powerful connections, as he was related to the first wife of the Emperor Claudius.

THE INVASION

Plautius led c.40,000 men in the invasion of Britain in AD43. The invasion almost failed before it began though: his soldiers

Richborough was one of Plautius' captured sites

were so afraid to set sail for barbaric Britain that the Emperor had to send his freedman, Narcissus, to shame them into obeying orders. Once in Britain, Plautius' army smashed through the south of Britain and reached Colchester, where Plautius waited with his army for Claudius to arrive to make a triumphal entry.

PLAUTIUS' ACHIEVEMENT

By the end of his governorship – a mere three years – all Britain south of a line between the Severn estuary and the Trent estuary had been conquered. The Fosse Way, a Roman road running from Exeter in Devon, through Leicester in the midlands and northwards to Lincoln, roughly marked this limit.

 DID YOU KNOW?
The Emperor Claudius granted Plautius an 'ovation' (a celebratory public procession back in Rome) for his conquest of Britain. He was the last Roman general ever to be allowed such glory: from then on, only Emperors would enjoy such praise.

AGRICOLA

 FULL NAME: Gnaius Julius Agricola | DATE OF GOVERNORSHIP: AD77/78–
AD83/84 | EMPEROR DURING GOVERNORSHIP: Vespasian (AD69–AD79);
Titus (AD79–AD81; Domitian (AD81–AD96)
RELATED SITES: Forts in Wales

A seasoned soldier, Agricola held the post of governor for the
exceptionally long time of seven years, probably on account of his
lengthy and very vigorous campaign to subdue Britain's frontiers.

WALES SUBDUED

Agricola had previously commanded the
XX Legion in Wroxeter and, on becoming
governor, immediately in AD77/78 took
them into victorious action against the
troublesome Welsh tribe, the Ordovices.

THE NORTHERN CAMPAIGN

The next summer, Agricola
took the army north,
surveying new land, and
building forts as they went:
Elginhaugh near Edinburgh
and Fendoch near Perth
were his, as was the major supply
base at Red House near Corbridge in
Northumberland.

In AD80/81, Agricola's troops reached
the Forth and Clyde and, although Tacitus
records that it was an ideal frontier (50
years later the Antonine Wall would be
built here), the army's devotion to Rome's
glory pushed them on. His army won
the decisive battle of *Mons Graupius* (site
unknown) in AD83/84 and reached the
northeast point of *Caledonia* (Scotland).

 ## WEIRD AND WONDERFUL

Much of our knowledge
about Agricola comes from a
book written about him (in a
somewhat biased fashion) by
his son-in-law, the Roman
historian, Tacitus.

ROMANISING INFLUENCE

Agricola encouraged the use of
Latin and Roman ways, and he
occupied the 'rough men who
lived in scattered settlements' in
building more houses, temples and other
public buildings by praising enthusiasm and
harassing those who were reluctant.

THE PRICE OF SUCCESS

Tacitus claimed Emperor Domitian
(AD81–AD96) was jealous of Agricola's
success and withdrew him from Britain.
Nonetheless, a monumental triumphal
arch celebrating the conquest of Britain
was built at Richborough, honouring the
Emperor and the work of Agricola.

NEPOS

FULL NAME: Aulus Platorius Nepos
DATE OF GOVERNORSHIP: AD122–AD125
EMPEROR DURING GOVERNORSHIP: Hadrian (AD117–AD138)
RELATED SITES: Hadrian's Wall

Nepos was governor of Britain when Hadrian's Wall was built between c.AD122 and AD126. As governor, he commanded the army and masterminded the construction of this military and political frontier.

NEPOS' CREDENTIALS

Nepos enjoyed the personal friendship of the Emperor Hadrian, and they had served together as joint consuls in Rome in AD119. Nepos came with military expertise and arrived with the *VI Victrix* Legion, fresh from their post in Lower Germany where he had been governor. Based in York, they boosted the manpower that had been lost when *IX Hispana* Legion left Britain in c.AD108.

A MONUMENTAL WORK

Nepos was ordered to build Hadrian's

As governor Nepos engineered the building of Hadrian's Wall

Wall, and a number of inscriptions linked with the building of the Wall and its forts refer to him as *propraetor* (chief administrator of a province, ie governor). To build the wall, Nepos made use of all three legions who were in Britain at the time (*II Augusta*, *VI Victrix* and *XX Valeria Victrix*) and a unit from the *Classis Britannica*.

A COSTLY BUSINESS

Nepos spent a vast fortune on Hadrian's Wall. Even before it was completed, the Wall had to be redesigned to be built quicker, using less stone and less manpower. Nepos left Britain in AD126, as the work was nearing completion. We know he fell out with the Emperor Hadrian – perhaps the building work was just too expensive. His fate is unknown...

IF YOU LIKED THIS...
Visit Hadrian's Wall and try to spot the narrowing that was a direct result of the cost cutting made during the building. It is visible above the first couple of stone courses and can be seen in many places but especially at Planetrees near Wall (Tynedale).

ALBINUS

FULL NAME: Decimus Clodius Albinus
DATE OF GOVERNORSHIP: AD191/2–AD197
EMPEROR DURING GOVERNORSHIP: Commodus (AD180–AD192);
Septimius Severus (AD193–AD211) | RELATED SITES: Vindolanda

Albinus was a governor who had ambition beyond his rank. He took the British army into Gaul to challenge Severus for imperial power but in his absence, northern Britain was ruined by a revolt.

A POTENTIAL EMPEROR

Albinus arrived in Britain as governor at roughly the same time (AD192) that Emperor Commodus was murdered by his own bodyguard. The imperial command was up for sale to any general who paid their army enough – and Albinus had three legions and numerous auxiliary troops behind him. Although Septimius Severus (governor in Germany) commanded 16 legions, a governor of Britain was a sufficient threat and Septimius offered to name Albinus as *Caesar* (a kind of junior co-Emperor) and thus make him his heir. While Severus fought Niger (governor of Syria) for dominance, Albinus remained in Britain.

NORTHERN BRITAIN REBELS

In AD194, Severus named his own son *Caesar,* and Albinus realised that he had been tricked. He proclaimed himself

Emperor and took much of Britain's troops to Gaul to challenge Severus.

This left Britain with minimal military force and manpower, leaving it open to attack from northern tribes (see p.57).

IF YOU LIKED THIS...

Visit Vindolanda just south of Hadrian's Wall: the stone fort that is visible now was built during the repairs following the *Maeatae* and *Caledonii* revolt.

ALBINUS' LEGACY

In AD197, Albinus committed suicide when Severus defeated his army near Lyons. Severus sent a new governor, Lupus, to buy off the *Maeatae* as a delaying tactic while extensive repairs were made to the damage done during the revolt.

Albinus' reign was not successful and he eventually committed suicide

SENECIO

 FULL NAME: Lucius Alfenus Senecio
DATE OF GOVERNORSHIP: AD205/207–c.AD208/9
EMPEROR DURING GOVERNORSHIP: Septimius Severus (AD193–AD211)
RELATED SITES: Vindolanda; Housesteads, Chester, Birdoswald and Corbridge

Senecio worked on the immense campaign of rebuilding the military forts and outposts in northern England. He then pushed Rome northwards again, beyond Hadrian's Wall.

Senecio commandeered the rebuilding of many destroyed Roman forts

BRITAIN: A STEPPING STONE

Senecio was posted to Britain in the early years of the third century. He was an example of the mobility of Roman officers: born in North Africa, at the southernmost edges of the Roman Empire, he had served as consul in Rome and been governor of Syria in AD200 before being sent to the northern limits of the empire.

RESTORATION WORK

Senecio inherited a Britain that had been savaged in the north by the tribes from north of Hadrian's Wall. Towns and forts, and the Wall itself, had been damaged and even destroyed. Inscribed stones from many northern sites record Senecio's restoration of several forts along Hadrian's Wall and beyond it, as well as of several outlying forts. This was the age of great Roman military rebuilding in northern Britain.

 DID YOU KNOW?

It was probably during Senecio's governorship that Emperor Severus split Britain into two provinces, *Britannia Superior* and *Britannia Inferior* to stop any governor of Britain wielding the kind of military power Albinus had enjoyed (see p.77).

SENECIO'S CAMPAIGNS

However, tribes on the northern border seem to have caused trouble in AD206/7 and Senecio's campaigns against them, although initially successful, stirred up the *Caledonii* league of tribes, who surged over Hadrian's wall, raided Roman towns and killed civilians as well as Roman soldiers.

Senecio asked the Emperor Septimius Severus for reinforcements. The Emperor himself chose to intervene and brought his two sons on a campaign into Scotland to punish the rebels and build prestige (see p.26).

CONSTANTINE I

FULL NAME: Constantine I (Constantine the Great)
EMPEROR DURING GOVERNORSHIP: AD306–AD337
RELATED SITES: York

When Emperor Constantius died in York in AD306, his soldiers proclaimed his son, Constantine, as the Western Roman Emperor. He used his position to aim towards total power throughout the Empire.

IMPERIAL POTENTIAL

Governors of Britain were directly answerable to the highest authority, the Emperor. However, in the late third century, the empire was split so that two men ruled the West and another two ruled the East (both partnerships consisting of a senior *augustus* and a junior *Caesar*). Constantius, Constantine's father, was *augustus* of the Western Roman Empire and once he had suppressed British rebel emperors in AD296 he was fully in command of the army in the Britain too.

CONSTANTINE TAKES CHARGE

Constantine joined his father in Britain in AD305 as he campaigned against the Picts beyond Hadrian's Wall. When his father died in AD306, the soldiers declared Constantine the *augustus*. Although there were other candidates for the title, those battles took place in Europe and Britain now enjoyed a time of peace and prosperity.

ULTIMATE POWER

Constantine continued to compete for imperial power. It was during this civil war that Constantine converted to Christianity and declared it to be the state religion. The Edict of Milan guaranteed religious tolerance and Christian symbols could be openly (if cautiously, as in Lullingstone) displayed. In AD324, Constantine became sole ruler of the entire Empire: the Empire was, once again, united under one man.

DID YOU KNOW?
The modern statue of Constantine in York stands near the spot where it is believed Constantine was proclaimed Emperor.

The statue of Emperor Constantine in York

THE ROMAN ARMY IN BRITAIN

The Roman soldier is the iconic image of Roman Britain: the legions, the armour, the eagle-topped standards and the forts are legendary. Their role in Roman Britain went further than military might though.

HOW WAS THE ARMY ORGANISED?

The Roman army was an efficient and strictly hierarchical organisation of legions that were each divided into 10 cohorts, each consisting of six *centuria* (centuries) of about 80 men (not 100 despite what the name suggests). These were further organised into close-knit teams of eight to 10 men. A legion was commanded by the *legatus legionis* (Legate of the Legion), a man of senatorial rank who answered directly to the governor of the province and to the Emperor himself.

DID YOU KNOW?

The writing tablets discovered at Vindolanda provide an insight into the daily lives of soldiers on the frontier: where men were stationed, discipline issues, private letters home for more socks, orders for food and beer supplies.

WHAT DID THE ARMY DO?

The army was used for far more than military conquest and law enforcement: soldiers could be assigned to the governor's staff as his bodyguard; their engineers were responsible for civil projects such as aqueducts, as well as fortifications; and they were the administrators of the military network that underpinned the entire province.

A high level of literacy in Latin was achieved throughout the ranks and soldiers often learned a trade, as masons, metalworkers, surveyors, etc. The army also produced much of its own iron, pottery, roof tiles and other materials.

WEIRD AND WONDERFUL

Soldiers might march 30km (20 miles) in one day. Each man wore full armour and carried 30kg (c.60lb) of kit, including his own shield, sword, dagger, helmet, blanket, tent pole, pick axe or mattock for digging camp and fort ramparts, as well as a spear. Soldiers also carried a bowl and cooking pan, water and food rations (for anything between three days and a fortnight), a leather kit bag and even a grinding stone for grain.

THE ARMY AFLOAT

The *Classis Britannica* was the fleet that linked Britain to the continent and Rome, bringing supplies, transporting troops, building forts and lighthouses (as at Dover)

Life as a Roman soldier came with strict terms and conditions

and even working and supplying essential iron. Evidence of the fleet's presence survives in workmen's identifying marks stamped on tiles and pipes, both on the south coast and on the shores on the northern frontier.

TERMS AND CONDITIONS

Soldiers signed up for 25 years' service, at the end of which they received a pension, a local plot of land to farm (next to other retired veterans) and Roman citizenship (which provided valuable legal rights). They could then marry, which they had been forbidden from doing during service.

Conditions of service eased during the third century: marrying was permitted and even illiterate soldiers could rise through the ranks.

A SKILLED FIGHTING FORCE

Roman legionaries wore articulated armour, the iconic helmet and fought with a short, stabbing sword.

However, the army in Britain probably consisted of twice as many support troops as regular legionaries. Using their specialist skills (the Batavian auxiliaries were 'superb horsemen' for example) and

their favoured weapons (eg slingshots or bows and arrows) and armour (chain mail, 'scales' or leather), they were well suited to fighting the dispersed guerrilla-style warfare that the Welsh and the Scottish tribes fought the Romans with.

Although originally drafted from other cultures, their pride in their skills and achievements attracted a cross-section of the nationalities of the Roman world. Their retirement package, however, did not include Roman citizenship.

A SPENT FORCE

Britain was conquered and held in the first century by four legions who built a powerful network of forts across the land. In AD89, though, one legion was withdrawn and by the fourth century there seem to have been only two legions left, the rest being deployed on the continent to defend the frontiers there.

 DID YOU KNOW?
Britain was one of the most heavily garrisoned of the Roman provinces, and almost half of the army in Britain was stationed at sites relating to Hadrian's Wall and the northern frontier.

Roman Legacy

Although the Romans left Britain in AD410, they left more than just ruins behind. Our landscape, buildings, art, literature, media and even the very words we use owe much to the Romans.

A SOLID HERITAGE

Ruins of Roman buildings and monuments are scattered across Britain and today we can walk around the remains of their homes and forts, bath houses and amphitheatres. We can admire their mosaics and hypocausts and even wall paintings. Museums enable us to get close to the things they owned – the pottery, inscriptions, tools and weapons, jewellery and clothes and even their personal letters.

A statue in the Classical style

Yet the Romans left behind far more than these material remains. They established a way of life that continues today: the towns they established, such as London, York and Bath are still centres of trade and administration.

These towns were linked by Roman roads that crossed the country. Many roads were followed for centuries, even when they were later built over by modern roads, so that they continued to influence the location of new settlements long after the Romans had gone (see p.84).

THE ROMANS LIVE ON

Aside from their physical impact, stories of the Romans in Britain are part of our culture: they have been told in books, in television documentaries and dramas and imaginatively on film (see p.96). The Roman gods (see p.70) and

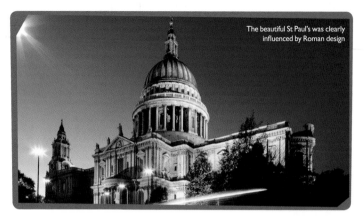

The beautiful St Paul's was clearly influenced by Roman design

myths appear in our statues and paintings and help to shape the images in our 'fantasy' tales.

More subtly – but more pervasively – the Romans' language, Latin, influenced the development of the English language and it continues to do so today (see p.85). Every time we speak or write, we owe a debt to the Romans who lived in Britain 2,000 years ago.

ROME REBORN

Rome's influence on our lives could have been minimal because Roman culture was largely lost after the Western Empire collapsed in the fifth century. In the 14th century AD, though, there was a re-awakening of interest in Classical (Greek and Latin) literature and arts. Everything Classical was searched out and became a central focus for all areas of architecture (see p.86), art, science, religion, politics, philosophy and all realms of intellectual thought. This was the Renaissance ('rebirth' of culture) and its effect was profound throughout Europe.

The studies carried out since then have enabled us to bring to life the ruins of Roman Britain and to see how the Roman rule has infiltrated every area of our lives ever since.

 DID YOU KNOW?
Until the mid-20th century, Latin was an essential qualification for entry into a medical or legal career, a job in the Church or entry to Oxford or Cambridge universities.

ROADS

> CURRENT STATUS: Often built over by later roads but many are lost
> DO WE STILL USE IT? Yes
> IN WHAT FORM? Some sections of modern roads follow the line of the
> Roman roads

The Roman army built a network of paved roads in Britain so that men and supplies could move quickly and easily. These roads united the province, and some modern roads and tracks still follow their routes.

The Fosse Way

WHAT WAS NEW ABOUT ROMAN ROADS

Some Roman roads were built on ancient track ways but the army created new solid roads to carry thousands of soldiers. Layers of large stones were covered by smaller stones and then compacted gravel or paving was added (*strata* meant 'paved' and gave us the word 'street'). They were cambered (angled) to ease drainage into the ditches on either side, and milestones lined the route.

DID YOU KNOW?
Contrary to popular belief, Roman roads were not always straight – they did go round impassable obstacles – but surveyors did plan them by direct line of sight where possible.

HIGHWAYS AND BYWAYS
Military roads radiated out from London and smaller roads linked sites to them and to each other. Over 16,000km (10,000 miles) of road were built in Britain and no farm was further than a few miles from one.

FOLLOWING THE ROADS
Many roads continued to be used after the Romans left but others were built over or worn away. Their routes can sometimes be tracked through the landscape but the main ones are buried beneath modern roads.

- **The Fosse Way:** from Exeter, through Bath, Gloucester and Leicester, to Lincoln. It has been largely adapted by modern roads.
- **Watling Street:** from Dover to London (the modern A2 road) and then west to Wroxeter (largely the modern A5).
- **Ermine Street:** this main road heading north from London to Lincoln is touched on by parts of the A10, A1 and A15 as well as many smaller roads.

 IF YOU LIKED THIS...
Some of the best examples of Roman roads can be seen at Blackstone Edge (Rishworth Moor near Manchester), Holtye (Sussex) and Wheeldale Moor (North Yorkshire).

LANGUAGE

> **CURRENT STATUS:** No one uses Latin as a native tongue, it is a 'dead' language
> **DO WE STILL USE IT?** Yes
> **IN WHAT FORM?** Pure Latin words, together with altered Latin words, appear frequently in English

The Romans spoke Latin. Although no one speaks it any more as their native tongue, Latin is used in English in virtually every area of our modern lives.

LATIN LIVES ON

We still use the Latin alphabet (now called the Roman alphabet) and many Roman words (such as *diploma*, *forum* and *status*) remain unchanged. Some words were later revived, while others were adopted for new uses, for example *virus* meant 'snake's poison' but is now used to refer to disease.

Latin is still part of our culture as can be seen on these £1 coins

More often, Latin words have been altered slightly, for example *colonia* became 'colony'. Latin words also prompted a hoard of English variations on the theme: *aqua* (as in Bath's Roman name, *aquae sulis*) meant 'water' and gave rise to 'aqueduct', 'aquarium' and 'aquatic', while the word *castrum* for army camp lingered in various forms in Roman town names, for example Doncaster, Colchester and Worcester.

A WEALTH OF LITERATURE

Roman literature was rediscovered in the Renaissance. Its histories, speeches, poetry and drama are still considered models of excellence and their stories, characters and themes have inspired English writers such as Chaucer, Shakespeare and Milton.

NEW LATIN

Latin was the international language of early science and all new concepts had to be published in Latin, meaning they required Latin names. These names were later anglicised, for example 'gravity' was originally *gravitas*. Even when theories and inventions could be presented in English, new words imitated Latin to give them authority, such as 'computers' which, originally were just glorified 'calculators' (*computare* was Latin for 'to count').

 IF YOU LIKED THIS...

You can explore the origins of English words by clicking on the Oxford English Dictionary's website, www.oed.com, and 'signing in'. You can register with your local library for a card and use your personal number on it.

Roman Legacy

ARCHITECTURE

 CURRENT STATUS: Ruins of Roman architecture, but many modern buildings
are imitations of their style
DO WE STILL USE IT? Yes
IN WHAT FORM? Columns, pediments, arches, vaults, inscriptions and statues

Romans built stone public buildings with columns and statues, arches
and vaults and our buildings still copy that style. At the other end of the
scale we also owe the simple idea of square houses to the Romans.

TOWNS, THEN AND NOW

The Romans introduced the concept of
towns to Britain and our landscape is now
populated with them, just as it was in
Roman times (see p.30). Modern towns
are not as regimented as the gridded
pattern used in Roman forts and towns,
but main streets often still converge onto
commercial centres, public offices and
cathedrals/churches, and side roads are
lined with properties that range from
residential homes to industrial units.

COLUMNS

Within our towns we have grand public
buildings that are fronted by columns
(fluted or straight) decorated with
rich Corinthian capitals at the top and
supporting triangular pediments (with or
without added sculptures). These are a
legacy of the Roman temples and basilicas
that provided the standard blueprint for
front elevations of public buildings then
and now.

Such buildings ceased to be built even
before the Romans left Britain (see p.28)
but they returned with the Renaissance
in Britain in the 16th century (Inigo Jones'
Banqueting House in Whitehall, for

example), when all things Classical were
back in favour.

 IF YOU LIKED THIS...
Check out the capitals (the
decorated tops of columns) of
buildings near you: they might
be leafy Corinthian capitals,
scrolled Ionic ones, or maybe
plain Doric, with just a plain
circular banding and/or collar.
These are all Classical styles.

UNDERNEATH THE ARCHES

Arches and vaults were invented by the
Romans: they used them in their drains
and bath houses to minimise the damage
to the roof due to damp (see p.38), while
monumental arches celebrated triumphs.
Arches are remarkably strong and some
substantial structures survived a long time,
for example the still-working Roman
aqueduct at Carlisle was proudly shown
to St Cuthbert in AD685.

STATUES

Many of our buildings and open spaces are
adorned with statues of leading figures in
Classical poses and on horseback, similar
to those carved by the Romans. We even

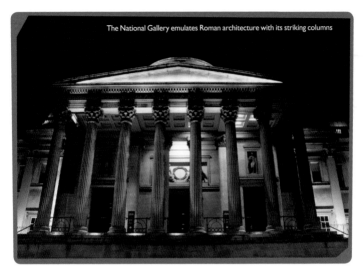

The National Gallery emulates Roman architecture with its striking columns

erect statues to remind us of our Roman past, such as Boudicca in her chariot in London, and Constantine enthroned in York.

WEIRD AND WONDERFUL

Roman statues were not the plain marble we appreciate today: they were painted in bright colours and they glistened in the sun with bright bronze or gold weapons or accessories.

INSCRIPTIONS

No Roman would dream of building an impressive building or monument without adding an inscription recording his name. Such inscriptions became fashionable again after the Renaissance, and when we include inscriptions today (eg 'This centre was opened by'), we still carve them in stone.

HOME SWEET HOME

The most fundamental architectural legacy of the Romans is perhaps the simplest: our square and rectangular houses and buildings. Without the Romans, we might still be living in the style that had been used for thousands of years before their arrival – the round house.

IF YOU LIKED THIS...

Take a good look around your local town and see how many columns, statues and arches there are: St Paul's Cathedral and the statue of Victory outside Buckingham Palace; the columns in the Royal Crescent in Bath; or even the arches beneath railway lines and the columns inside local churches.

TOP 10 ROMAN FINDS

1 CARLISLE ARMOUR

Where found: Carlisle

Dating from: c.AD122

What is it? Several very rare articulated pieces of Roman armour, exceptionally preserved in waterlogged conditions, complete with copper-alloy rivets and leather backing.

Visit it: Tullie House Museum, Carlisle

2 PEDIMENT FROM ROMAN BATHS AT BATH

Where found: Bath

Dating from: Late first century AD

What is it? This stone carving from the temple pediment reveals the remarkable blending of Roman and local culture and styles.

Visit it: The Roman Baths, Bath, Somerset

3 RIBCHESTER HOARD

Where found: Ribchester, Lancashire

Dating from: c.AD120

What is it? A hoard of military metalwork giving a glimpse into military kit, including a complete Roman bronze ceremonial helmet, found in a storage box beneath a barrack block.

Visit it: British Museum

4 VINDOLANDA WRITING TABLETS

Where Found: Vindolanda

Dating from: c.AD100

What is it? The writing on these small, thin pieces of wood supplies a wealth of information about the army and personal lives at Vindolanda.

Visit them: British Museum and Vindolanda's Museum

5 CEREMONIAL HELMET
Where found: Crosby Garrett, Cumbria
Dating from: late first/early second century AD
What is it? An exceptional Roman bronze two-piece ceremonial helmet and facemask.
Visit it: Sold to private owner.

6 HOXNE HOARD
Where found: Hoxne, Suffolk
Dating from: Fifth century AD
What is it? Over 15,000 gold and silver coins, gold jewellery and items of silver tableware including a fine silver tigress.
Visit it: British Museum

7 FROME COIN HOARD
Where found: Frome, Somerset
Dating from: AD253–AD305
What is it? Over 52,000 Roman silver or bronze coins (including some from Carausius' rule) in a ceramic pot – one of the largest coin hoards in Britain.
Visit it: British Museum

8 COINAGE OF TASCIOVANUS AND MOULDS
Where found: Southern England
Dating from: Pre-AD43
What is it? Pre-Roman coins of the British tribal King, Tasciovanus. These coins provide evidence for early Roman influence. A mould for blank coins has also been found.
Visit them: St Albans' Verulamium Museum

9 THETFORD TREASURE
Where found: Thetford, Norfolk
Dating from: mid to late fourth century AD
What is it? A collection of high status gold and silver items including jewellery and spoons displaying emblems of the pagan cult Faunus.
Visit it: British Museum

10 MILDENHALL SILVER TABLEWARE HOARD
Where found: Mildenhall, Suffolk
Dating from: Fourth century
What is it? Major hoard of high-quality silver plate, including dishes, spoons, goblets, platters and ladles and the Great Dish (60.5cm/24 inches wide) decorated with Bacchic figures.
Visit it: British Museum

WHAT LIFE WAS LIKE AFTER THE ROMANS

When the Roman army left Britain in AD410, skills, money and manpower went with them. With no single power in charge, society broke down and memories of Rome began to fade.

A FOND FAREWELL

Britain's infrastructure had been created and maintained by the Romans for 400 years. Britain was not eager to discard life as a Roman province: as late as AD407, Constantine III was proclaimed Emperor in Britain largely because his name harked back to the earlier days of Constantine I (see p.79). Similarly, when government links with Rome collapsed, late Roman administrative offices (such as 'vicar', 'deacon' and 'diocese') continued and would be adopted by the Christian church in the hope of continuing some kind of normality and law and order in an uncertain world.

DID YOU KNOW?
The stories of King Arthur are said to be from the time after the Romans left Britain. His role is often portrayed as that of a civilising king in a world falling into chaos.

A RETURN TO THE LAND

The departure of the army meant that no money arrived from Rome to pay the soldiers. This loss of cash flow in Britain affected trade and the towns, forts and villas that had been dependent on this trade dwindled away. Many people returned to farming.

WEIRD AND WONDERFUL
As villas ceased to have any meaning as status symbols, they became nothing more than agricultural farms: the fine mosaic floor in the villa at Dinnington in Somerset was reduced to serving as a convenient threshing floor, and a corn-drying oven was cut into Brading villa's mosaics.

The ability to replace or repair fine goods or stone buildings was lost. As the material memories (buildings, tools and luxury goods) collapsed or broke, the Romans faded from living memory.

Stone buildings were no longer maintained after the Romans left

DID YOU KNOW?

Knowledge of skills and crafts were lost to the point that the silted-up baths in Bath were thought to have been the 'works of giants', as claimed in *The Ruin*, an eighth century Old English poem.

Anglo-Saxons and Vikings moved into the fertile lands of Britain but (apart from a few later Viking settlements such as York/Jorvik) they were localised centres: they had little interest in bringing regions together for sustained mutual benefit. Integrated town life had collapsed.

IF YOU LIKED THIS...

Visit the Jorvik centre in York. Compare their reconstruction of this pinnacle of life under the Vikings – the timber houses and lack of stonework – with the stone public buildings in town life under the Romans.

TATTERED REMNANTS

The economy that had been fuelled by taxation and military wages began to shrink. Hoards, such as those at Hoxne, Mildenhall and Thetford, began to be buried in Britain: were they being hidden from barbarian attack, or merely stored for safekeeping for a brighter future? The hoards deteriorated from collections of artistic quality into beaten items, valued for the sheer weight of their metals and materials alone.

IF YOU LIKED THIS...

Compare the silver dishes and fine workmanship in the Mildenhall Treasure (fourth century) with the later (10th century) Vale of York treasure (previously known as the Harrogate Hoard) which is made up of broken and twisted silver, valued only for its weight.

A NEW CENTRE

Without the Romans at the helm, Britain needed a new focal point to hold society together: the church stepped into the void. The chronicler Gildas (born c.AD493) and later writers reveal that educated Latin culture continued in monasteries into the sixth century. The Church also provided connections between religious centres (including European ones) as well as a voice of moral authority.

THE ROMAN LEGACY TODAY

The Romans transformed Britain. Their impact is still felt in our modern lives: in the very words we speak but also in our buildings and in the landscape around us. Today, we can visit the evidence of their time here throughout Britain: we can marvel at the forts and the strength of their military might, admire their craftsmanship in jewellery and metalwork, and read their letters and curses to get a glimpse of what was important to them. While walking among the ruins we can share not just their space but something of their lives too.

GLOSSARY

AMPHORA
The two-handled pottery jar used by Romans to store anything from wine to olives. They usually had a pointed base and were sealed by a wax plug and the contents were marked on the side or on a label.

APODYTERIUM
The changing room at the Roman baths. It contained open slots to leave your clothes but theft was a constant problem, see p.39.

AUGUSTUS
Originally the title given by the Senate of Rome to Octavian when he became the first Emperor of Rome. In the second century *augustus* was the 'senior' Emperor alongside a 'junior' *Caesar.*

AUXILIARY
Auxiliary troops were made up of infantry and cavalry and used specific fighting skills such as sling shots or archery (see p.80).

BALLISTA
The heavy artillery of the Roman army: these huge catapult machines were often placed on bastions (tower platforms) on Roman town walls.

BASILICA
An imposing building used for judicial and administrative purposes in towns. It was built as one side of the forum (see p.30 on towns, and p.49 on Lincoln's basilica).

BRITANNIA
The Latin name for the Roman province of Britain. It included modern England and Wales, but only briefly and partially southern Scotland, and never Ireland.

CAESAR
Originally, the family name of Julius Caesar, whose great nephew was Augustus, the first Emperor of Rome, the name was used to address all Emperors. In the second century it was used as a title for a 'junior' Emperor (the senior being called *augustus*).

CALDARIUM
The hot room in the bath house. Its floor and walls were heated by a hypocaust system.

CALEDONIA
The name the Romans used for the regions occupied by the Scottish tribes, ie all of the area north of Hadrian's Wall.

CAPITAL
Roman columns would be topped by a piece of decorative stonework called a 'capital'. The Latin word was *capitalis* which meant 'of the head', ie the head or top of the column.

CIVITAS
The status granted to towns such as Silchester (p.33) that were administrative capitals for a region within a province.

CIVITATES
'Citizens' of Rome. This was a specific legal identity which was granted by Rome and

gave legal protection, including against capital and corporal punishments.

CLASSIS BRITANNICA
Latin for the 'British Fleet', a distinct unit of the Roman army in Britain. They were based at Roman towns and forts on the shore (such as Dover).

COHORT
A unit of the army, a cohort consisted of six centuries (units of 80 men).

COLONIA
A town, such as York (see p.44), that was first founded as a settlement of Roman army veterans, sometimes within the old demilitarised fort.

CORINTHIAN
An ornate style of stone capitals (tops) of columns used in architecture. The Corinthian style displayed curling leaves.

FORUM
The main commercial centre in a major town such as Caerwent (see p.42). It was an open area surrounded by colonnaded buildings.

FRIGIDARIUM
The cold room in the bath house, often including a cold plunge bath.

HYPOCAUST
The underfloor heating system that was fuelled by a fire outside the building: the heat travelled under the stone slab floors that were raised on pillars.

LEGATUS
Anyone chosen as a second-in-command, either to the governor or the Emperor. In Roman Britain it often referred to the commander of a legion.

LEGATUS LEGIONIS
The 'Legate of the Legion' was the commanding officer for a legion. He answered to the governor of the province and to the Emperor.

LEGION
A unit of the army, consisting of 10 cohorts and comprising between 4,200 and 6,000 men.

LEGIONARY
A Roman soldier who belonged to a legion and who was a Roman Citizen with certain legal rights.

MACELLUM
A large public market area, usually selling food. These could be open air spaces or roofed over.

MANSIO
An overnight roadside lodge, built for Roman officials and those on Roman business who carried a 'pass' called a *diploma*.

MILECASTLES
These fortified gateways, each with accommodation for about a dozen soldiers, were built every mile along Hadrian's Wall.

MITHRAEUM

A temple to the god, Mithras. Its vaulted roof and aisled interior represented the cave in the story of Mithras (see p.71).

MUNICIPIUM

The status given to a provincial town such as St Albans (*Verulamium*) whose residents were granted 'Latin citizenship', a lesser type of Roman citizenship.

OPPIDA

The Latin word for 'towns' that Julius Caesar adopted to describe the fortified/ramparted settlement areas of pre-Roman Iron-Age Britain.

PALAESTRA

The open area that was the exercise yard for the bath house. Some in Britain (for example the one at Wroxeter, see p.47) were, unusually, roofed in.

PATRONAGE

The support of a higher-ranking Roman.

PEDIMENT

A low-pitched triangular stone gable on columns at the front of temples. It was often filled with sculptures of mythical figures. A modern example is the entrance of the British Museum.

PRAETORIUM

The residence of the commandant of the legion and his family. It was built as four wings around a courtyard.

PRINCIPIA

The headquarters in a fort. Located centrally, it housed the legion's standards and the sunken storeroom for the soldiers' wages.

PROCURATOR

An administrative post, held by a Roman citizen. The Imperial Procurator was responsible for the province's financial affairs.

PROPRAETOR

An official or officer who had the powers of a *praetor* (magistrate). It was a common title for the governor of a province such as Britain.

SAMIAN WARE POTTERY

Designer quality pottery from Samia in Gaul (France). It had a distinctive smooth, red finish that was finely decorated.

SESTERCES

A Roman unit of money used throughout the Empire. Its value varied through the centuries.

STANDARD

Every legion had its 'standard', a pole headed by the figure of an animal (usually an eagle) and bearing symbols of 'honours' won by the legion.

TEMENOS

A Greek word used by the Romans for the walled precinct that surrounded some temples. It was a sacred area and might contain more than one temple.

TEPIDARIUM

The warm room in the bath house.

TRIUMVIRATE

A political agreement between three men to rule Rome together during a turbulent time in Rome: Julius Caesar, Pompey and Crassus formed the First Triumvirate in 60BC.

VALLUM

A flat-bottomed ditch, often between ramparts in a defensive system of ditches and ramparts.

VENEER

A thin layer of material used to cover or front something: a veneer of marble faced some Roman buildings to give the impression of a solid marble structure.

VICUS

The unofficial settlement that grew up next to a Roman fort and which could became a thriving town, as at Lincoln (see p.49).

WATCHTOWERS

Two watchtowers were placed, a third of a mile apart, between each milecastle on Hadrian's Wall.

PICTURE CREDITS

Photographs are reproduced with the permission of the following:

Alamy/Powered by Light/Alan Spencer: p.51
Andrew Barclay (Flickr): p.25
©Andrew Hovell: p.33
Andy Hay (Flickr): p.68
©Bath & North East Somerset Council: p.38
Caesaris.com: p.11 top middle; p.77
©Canterbury Archaeological Trust Ltd: p.36
Carl Bavin-Flaste (Flickr): p.49
Charles D P Miller (Flickr): p.66
Chris Downer (geograph): p.29
Claire Parfrey (Flickr): p.8 top left; p.10 centre left; p.16
Colchester and Ipswich Museum Service: p.20
The Corinium Museum: p.46
Dave Crosby (Flickr): p.48
Devon & Somerset Microlight Club: p.18
Dreamstime.com, © Kmiragaya: p.6
©English Heritage Photo Library: p.43; p.46; p.61
The Ermine Street Guard: p.17; p.73 top
George Evans (geograph): p.84
©Gillian Hovell: p.4; p.9 centre left, centre right; p.19; p.24; p.40; p.44; p.58; p.64; p.71; p.79
Glen Bowman (Flickr): p.55
©Heidi Dennis: p.11 bottom middle; p.35
Helen Hovell: p.12
©Historic Scotland. Licensor www.scran.ac.uk: p.69
Holly Ivins: p.10 centre; p.39; p.73 bottom
Ira & Larry Goldberg Coins & Collectibles: p.10 top right

istock: Cover, p.5 top; p.8 top right; p.10 top left; p.15; p.26; p.37; p.50; p.75; p.80; p.85; p.87; p.88 centre
Jim Brophy: p.90
Jonathan Himoff (Flickr): p.9 centre right; p.89 centre left
Kevin Freeborn: p.7; p.10 bottom left; p.32; p.62; p.63
©Last Refuge/Robert Harding World Imagery/Corbis: p.74
©Liz Forrest: p.54
Loz Pycock (Flickr): p.11 bottom left; p.67
©National Museums Scotland. Licensor www.scran.ac.uk: p.23
Numismatic Bibliomania society (Flickr): p.89 centre right
Oglander Roman Trust: p.65
Rex harris (Flickr): p.11 top right; p.89 bottom
roman-britain.org: p.42
thinkstock: p.5 bottom; p.8 centre left, bottom; p.9 top, bottom; p.10 bottom right; p.11 top left, bottom right; p.14; p.21; p.28; p.41; p.45; p.56; p.57; p.60; p.70; p.76; p.78; p.82; p.83 top, bottom
Thunderchild7 (Flickr): p.59
©The Trustees of the British Museum: p.27; p.89 top left
Tyler Bell (Flickr): p.22
©Vindolanda Trust: p.8 centre right; p.88 bottom
Wessex Archaeology (Flickr): p.91

USEFUL SOURCES

WEBSITES

www.bbc.co.uk/history/ancient/romans

www.bbc.co.uk/radio4/features/in-our-time/archive
(Radio 4's excellent archive of their *In Our Time* programmes includes experts' lively discussions on items like Boudicca, pre-Roman Celts and Rome's decline.)

www.britishmuseum.org

www.english-heritage.org.uk

www.nationaltrust.org.uk

www.nts.org.uk

www.roman-britain.org

www.romanbritain.freeserve.co.uk

BOOKS

Agricola, Tacitus (Penguin Classics, 2010)

Asterix in Britain, René Goscinny and Albert Uderzo (Asterix Orion Hardcover, 2004)

A History of Roman Britain, Peter Salway (Oxford, 2001)

The OS Map of Roman Britain (Ordnance Survey, 2001)

Roman Britain: A New History, Guy de la Bédoyère, (Thames and Hudson, 2010)

Roman Britain: A Very Short Introduction, Peter Salway (Oxford, 2000)

FILMS

Centurion (2010): action film imagining Roman struggles against the Picts in AD117.

The Eagle (2011): historical epic, loosely adapted from Rosemary Sutcliff's book *The Eagle of the Ninth*.

I, Claudius (1976): BBC TV drama starring Derek Jacobi about the Imperial life in Rome that influenced Claudius.

The Last Legion (2007): Colin Firth and Ben Kingsley star in this fictitious blend of legends from the end of the Western Roman Empire.

What the Romans Did for Us (2000): six episode TV documentary with Adam Hart-Davis.